hamlyn
Quick**Cook**

hamlyn
QuickCook
Italian

Joy Skipper

Every dish, three ways – you choose!
30 minutes | 20 minutes | 10 minutes

An Hachette UK Company
www.hachette.co.uk

First published in Great Britain in 2012 by Hamlyn,
a division of Octopus Publishing Group Ltd
Endeavour House, 189 Shaftesbury Avenue
London WC2H 8JY
www.octopusbooks.co.uk

ISBN 978-0-600-62492-9

A CIP catalogue record for this book is available from the British Library

Printed and bound in China

10 9 8 7 6 5 4 3 2 1

Both metric and imperial measurements are given for the recipes. Use one set of
measures only, not a mixture of both.

Standard level spoon measurements are used in all recipes
1 tablespoon = 15 ml
1 teaspoon = 5 ml

Ovens should be preheated to the specified temperature. If using a fan-assisted oven,
follow the manufacturer's instructions for adjusting the time and temperature. Grills
should also be preheated.

This book includes dishes made with nuts and nut derivatives. It is advisable for
those with known allergic reactions to nuts and nut derivatives and those who may
be potentially vulnerable to these allergies, such as pregnant and nursing mothers,
invalids, the elderly, babies and children, to avoid dishes made with nuts and nut oils.

It is also prudent to check the labels of preprepared ingredients for the possible
inclusion of nut derivatives.

The Department of Health advises that eggs should not be consumed raw. This book
contains some dishes made with raw or lightly cooked eggs. It is prudent for more
vulnerable people such as pregnant and nursing mothers, invalids, the elderly, babies
and young children to avoid uncooked or lightly cooked dishes made with eggs.

Contents

Introduction

30 20 10 – Quick, Quicker, Quickest

This book offers a new and flexible approach to meal-planning for busy cooks and lets you choose the recipe option that best fits the time you have available. Inside you will find 360 dishes that will inspire you and motivate you to get cooking every day of the year. All the recipes take a maximum of 30 minutes to cook. Some take as little as 20 minutes and, amazingly, many take only 10 minutes. With a bit of preparation, you can easily try out one new recipe from this book each night and slowly you will build a wide and exciting portfolio of recipes to suit your needs.

How Does it Work?

Every recipe in the QuickCook series can be cooked one of three ways – a 30-minute version, a 20-minute version or a super-quick and easy 10-minute version. At the beginning of each chapter you'll find recipes listed by time. Choose a dish based on how much time you have and turn to that page.

You'll find the main recipe in the middle of the page with a beautiful photograph and two time-variations below.

If you enjoy the dish, you can go back and cook the other time options. If you liked the 20-minute Bacon Carbonara (see pages 102–103), but only have 10 minutes to spare, then you'll find a way to cook it using cheat ingredients or clever shortcuts.

If you love the ingredients and flavours of the 10-minute Herb Butter Squid (see pages 156–157), why not try something more substantial such as the 20-minute Spiced Squid with Chickpeas, or be inspired to cook a more elaborate meal using similar ingredients, such as the 30-minute Crispy Squid. Alternatively, browse through all of the 360 delicious recipes, find something that takes your eye and then cook the version that fits your time frame.

Or, for easy inspiration, turn to the gallery on pages 12–19 to get an instant overview by themes, such as Vegetarian Delights and Fruity Favourites.

QuickCook Online

To make life even easier, you can use the special code on each recipe page to email yourself a recipe card for printing, or email a text-only shopping list to your phone. Go to www.hamlynquickcook.com and enter the recipe code at the bottom of each page.

ITA-SOUP-CEX

QuickCook Italian

Italian food is so much more than you first imagine. Pizza, pasta and risotto are very well known throughout Europe, and have been copied and reproduced (never at the same standard) for many years. But Italy has many different regions, each with its own special cuisine and eating habits.

The food in Italy has always been very important in society. The cuisine developed its diversity after the fall of the Roman Empire brought about a country of individually governed states that each had its own identity and hence its own traditions and cuisines. The true food of Italy is found in remote villages where little has changed over the centuries. There you will find country markets filled with produce that has been grown and picked by the person that is selling on the stall.

Geography also plays a large part in defining culinary styles, with around 1,500 miles of coastline where fish and seafood abound, plus the Apennine mountain range that forms the backbone of Italy. The length of the country gives rise to a huge variety of styles, with the north being more Germanic, cold-weather cooking using butter, and the south using more Mediterranean ingredients, with copious amounts of olive oil.

Other countries have also influenced Italian cuisine. The food of the north-west region of Italy bordering France closely resembles French cuisine (again using butter instead of olive oil), whereas the region bordering Austria in the north-east has Austrian influences and is known for its rich broths and smoked meats. Food in the south relies more heavily on seafood, with anchovies, sardines and swordfish being widely used. Although the various regions serve different styles of food there are some staple foods that are eaten across the country: pasta, risotto and olive oil all feature extensively throughout Italy.

An Italian Meal

Italian cuisine starts with breakfast of a simple pastry and cup of coffee. Lunch is the main meal of the day and comprises several courses. Italian meals may last one or two hours, or even longer. Antipasti comes before a main meal and could consist of a platter of local meats, cheeses, stuffed peppers and local breads. The first course is normally pasta, soup or a rice dish such as risotto. The second course is usually meat, poultry or fish, and with this a side dish of potato, vegetables or salad is served. Desserts or cheeses follow. Then the whole thing is rounded off by a good, strong Italian coffee.

Italians identify good food with fresh ingredients, and this also highlights the different regional dishes, as what grows well in Tuscany may not grow well in southern Italy. And although some ingredients are now available all year round, Italians prefer to create dishes using only seasonal ingredients. Regional recipes tend towards simplicity as they use only those ingredients that can be grown or sourced locally.

A Healthy Lifestyle

People who live in countries that border the Mediterranean Sea are known to have one of the healthiest diets in the world – locally grown fruit and vegetables, freshly caught fish and seafood, and everything drizzled with delicious olive oil (the Italian-Mediterranean diet is not low in fat, but olive oil is at least a healthy fat). Italians also take time to eat, enjoying family meals at a table – meal times are still very much a social occasion, all of which results in a healthier nation.

QuickCook Techniques and Tips

Creative cookery is not only possible for those who have plenty of time to spend in the kitchen. The recipes in this book can be cooked in no time at all using healthy, delicious ingredients and with a little help from a well-stocked storecupboard. The following pages feature a wide range of quick-to-prepare yet delicious Italian dishes, great for those of us who have a busy lifestyle. These recipes offer huge scope to be inventive in the quickest possible time. Using condiments, seasonings, herbs and spices can liven up your dining experience, giving you an opportunity to cook and eat a glorious palette of flavours, colours and textures.

A well-equipped kitchen will help you to save time when preparing your meals. A couple of good saucepans of different sizes, a frying pan and a wok are all essentials, and you will find lots of uses for a good-quality pestle and mortar. A salad spinner speeds up salad washing, and accurate kitchen scales will help to ensure successful results. A food processor or blender is a must for preparing soups and sauces.

QuickCook Ingredients

Stock up your storecupboard before you begin to travel through the varied and wonderful world of Italian cookery. With a good assortment of ingredients in your larder you can choose from a wider selection of speedy recipes to cook at a moment's notice.

pasta, polenta, rice and pulses
Pasta is eaten throughout Italy. It can be made with or without egg, using durum wheat and/or soft wheat flour and eaten fresh or dried. Italians have strong opinions regarding which pasta to use with which sauce, and different regions favour different combinations.

Polenta is a coarsely ground corn flour that is cooked in water to the consistency of mashed potatoes and served with meat or squid in a sauce. Once cold, soft polenta sets into a rigid block that can be topped with other ingredients and grilled. Instant polenta takes just five minutes to cook.

Risotto rice comes in three varieties – arborio, carnaroli and vialone nano – all of which are grown in Italy's Po Valley. Stirring risotto as it cooks helps the grains release their starch and makes the final result deliciously creamy.

Borlotti beans, cannellini beans, chickpeas and lentils are the backbone of many Italian soups, stews and salads. When cooking them from dry, they will need soaking overnight in cold water. Canned pulses, rinsed, can be used if time is short.

cheese and ham
Italy is world famous for its many different types of cheese. Parmesan, perhaps the most celebrated of all, is a hard cows' milk cheese made in northern Italy that is used extensively in Italian cooking. Grana Padano is similar but more economical. Pecorino, made in central and southern Italy from sheep's milk, is another popular choice. Fontina is a mild cheese from Piedmont, which melts evenly and smoothly, making it perfect for cooking. Of the blue cheeses, tasty Gorgonzola and milder, creamier dolcelatte are both used in creamy pasta sauces.

Softer cheeses also abound in Italy. Mozzarella can be made from cows' or water buffalos' milk; use the cows' milk variety in cooking, but choose creamier buffalo mozzarella if you are planning to eat it fresh. Ricotta, which has many culinary uses, is a naturally low-fat soft cheese made from the whey left over from cheese making. Mascarpone, which is famously used in the classic dessert, tiramisu, is a thick, full-fat cream cheese with a rich, smooth texture and mild flavour.

Prosciutto is a dry-cured Italian ham, the most famous variety being Parma ham. It can be thinly sliced and served uncooked as an antipasti, but is equally versatile as a salad ingredient, or when used to wrap fillets of fish, meat or chicken.

tomatoes
There is an abundance of tomatoes of every different kind available in Italy in summer and each variety has its own use. San Marzano plum tomatoes are prized for making sauces, and are the variety most commonly used in cans. Passata is smooth, raw puréed tomatoes sold bottled or in cartons to use in cooking.

mushrooms
Porcini, chanterelles and girolles are the most widely available wild mushrooms in Italy. During their short season in late summer and autumn, they are eaten raw in salads, pan-fried with garlic and stirred into pasta, eaten on bruschette or polenta, used in risottos or served with steak. Any other time of the year, Italians rely on dried mushrooms that need soaking in hot water before cooking.

anchovies, capers and olives
These storecupboard favourites are invaluable for adding extra flavour to many Italian dishes. Anchovies are most commonly used in southern cooking, and can be bought fresh or preserved in salt or oil. Capers are small flower buds that are preserved in salt or brine. Olives are a staple of Italian cuisine, and are most often enjoyed as part of an antipasti, though they are also used to flavour everything from pizzas to pasta.

olive oil and vinegar
Olive oil comes in different grades: extra-virgin olive oil is made from the first cold pressing of olives and is rich in flavour, whereas regular, commercially processed olive oil is much milder. As frying and sautéing can destroy the taste and fragrance of olive oil, use a cheaper, milder olive oil for cooking and reserve the more expensive variety for uncooked dishes.

Red wine vinegar is commonly used in Italy for both dressing salads and cooking. Sweet and syrupy balsamic vinegar, made in Modena, is also popular, and just a few drops are enough to enliven a salad, sauce or even a bowl of fresh strawberries.

Vegetarian Delights

Delicious meat-free treats – definitely not just for the vegetarians.

Stuffed Courgettes 32

Asparagus Frittata 40

Mozzarella and Spinach Stuffed Pancakes 52

Savoy Cabbage and Parmesan Soup 66

Aubergine Melts 68

Wild Mushroom Crostini 72

Chickpea and Chestnut Soup 86

Stuffed Mushrooms 92

Mushroom Risotto 104

Broccoli and Chilli Orecchiette 114

Sweetcorn and Spinach Polenta 130

Pea and Spring Onion Linguine 150

Fruity Favourites

Packed with nutritious fruit, here are some delicious ways to achieve your five a day.

Pear, Walnut and
Gorgonzola Salad 60

Cream of Pumpkin and
Apple Soup 74

Saffron Scallops with Apple
and Pistachio Purée 180

Lemon and Rosemary Pork
with Cannellini Bean Salad 206

Polenta-Crusted Pork with
Pear and Rocket Salad 214

Honey, Mustard and
Lemon Lamb 216

Pear and Mascarpone
Pancakes 242

Roasted Amaretti Peaches 244

Sweet Ricotta and
Raspberries 246

Pear Strudel 256

Creamy Peach and Banana
Smoothies 266

Amaretto Apricot
Dessert 274

Summer Specials

Great ideas for al-fresco dining, Italian style.

2 Sicilian Potato Salad 34

3 Wild Mushroom Tart 56

2 Griddled Swordfish with Salsa Verde 158

3 Mackerel with Beetroot and Potato Salad 162

1 Prawn and Tomato Salad 184

2 Pan-Fried Red Mullet with Green Beans 186

3 Marinated Sardines 190

1 Tuna and Cannellini Bean Salad 192

1 Lamb-Stuffed Pitta 208

1 Watermelon and Pineapple with Sambuca 258

2 Apple and Parmesan Tartlets 264

3 Honeyed Fig Fool 270

Classics

Our selection of Italian classics, just like Mama used to make!

Peperonata 30

Potato Gnocchi 100

Bacon Carbonara 102

Fiorentina Pizza 106

Spaghetti Bolognese with Griddled Cherry Tomatoes 116

Spaghetti Puttanesca 136

Italian Fish and Seafood Stew 164

Beef Carpaccio 200

Creamy Veal Escalopes 224

Tiramisu 250

Zabaglioni 252

Biscotti 268

Entertaining

Make stressful dinner parties a thing of the past with these stunning, but easy dishes.

Antipasti with Breadsticks 24

Crab Linguine 110

Pea and Mint Risotto 118

Saffron Risotto 124

Rigatoni with Mussels and Courgettes 132

Herb Butter Squid 156

Monkfish Wrapped in Prosciutto with Lentils and Spinach 172

Creamy Mussels with Pancetta 182

Lamb and Olive Stew 198

Veal with Prosciutto and Sage 204

Mixed Peel Cassata 276

Chocolate Amaretti Puddings 278

Light and Healthy

Enjoy the fresh and light flavours of the Mediterranean.

Italian Vegetable Kebabs 54

Borlotti Bean and Roasted Red Pepper Bruschetta 62

Grilled Radicchio with Pancetta 76

Broad Bean and Mint Soup 84

Fusilli with Watercress, Raisins and Pine Nuts 142

Stuffed Mussels 160

Prawn and Cannellini Bean Salad 168

Tuna with Cannellini Beans and Roasted Red Pepper 174

Baked Trout with Olives 176

Sea Bass Fillets with Lentil Salad 178

Roman Chicken with Peppers 218

Smoked Duck Breast Salad 234

Ways with Cheese

Where would Italian food be without cheese, in all its varied forms?

Parmesan Breadsticks 26

Roasted Red Pepper and Goats' Cheese Salad 38

Spinach and Pecorino Balls with Tomato Sauce 42

Baked Ricotta 48

Baked Fennel and Gorgonzola 70

Cheese-Stuffed Onions 78

Parmesan Crisps 82

Fettucine with Dolcelatte and Spinach 122

Cheese and Spinach Calzones 134

Cheese Gnocchi with Spinach and Walnuts 146

Chicken Parmesan 202

Ricotta Pancakes with Oranges and Figs 272

Ways with Tomatoes

A classic Italian ingredient, conjuring up the tastes of the sun.

Roast Tomato Soup 46

Broad Beans with Anchovies and Tomatoes 50

Tomato, Basil and Mozzarella Salad 58

Panzanella 80

Penne Arrabbiata 120

Tomato Risotto 128

Aubergine and Courgette Ratatouille Pizzas 138

Margherita Pizza 148

Tuna in Tomato and Caper Sauce 166

Chilli Cod in Tomato Sauce 170

Meatballs with Tomato Sauce and Spaghetti 222

Chicken BLT 226

QuickCook

Soups, Salads and Light Bites

Recipes listed by cooking time

30

20

 Antipasti with Breadsticks

Serves 4

100 g (3½ oz) marinated olives
75 g (3 oz) chargrilled marinated
  artichokes
50 g (2 oz) chargrilled peppers
50 g (2 oz) sun-dried tomatoes
50 g (2 oz) marinated anchovies
100 g (3½ oz) prosciutto
100 g (3½ oz) salami
220 g (7½ oz) mozzarella cheese
6 tablespoons extra-virgin
  olive oil
4 tablespoons aged balsamic
  vinegar
grissini breadsticks, to serve

- Arrange the ingredients on a large platter or board. When ready to eat, pour the olive oil and balsamic vinegar into separate bowls for dipping.

- Serve the Antipasti with grissini breadsticks.

2 Smoked Mackerel Bruschetta

Cut a large baguette into 8 slices. Brush each one with olive oil, and cook under a preheated hot grill on both sides, until toasted and golden. Mix together 225 g (7½ oz) smoked mackerel with 6 chopped plum tomatoes, 2 tablespoons toasted pine nuts, the juice of 1 lemon and 1 tablespoon chopped parsley. Stir ½ teaspoon creamed horseradish into 175 g (6 oz) cream cheese and spread the cheese on to each slice of bruschetta. Top with the mackerel mixture and serve.

3 Assorted Crostini

Cut a thin baguette into 12 slices. Brush each one with olive oil and cook under a hot grill on both sides, until toasted and golden. Rub each slice with a garlic clove. Halve, core and deseed 1 red pepper and cook, cut side down, under a preheated hot grill, until the skin turns black. Place in a bowl, cover with clingfilm and leave until cool enough to handle, then peel away the blackened skin. Cut the peppers into strips and place on 4 of the crostinis. Top with 50 g (2 oz) crumbled goats' cheese and ½ teaspoon chopped thyme leaves. Chop 1 tomato with ½ teaspoon capers and 4–5 basil leaves. Spoon this over another 4 of the crostini and drizzle with 1 tablespoon extra-virgin olive oil. Top the remaining 4 crostini with 4 slices of prosciutto and 1 teaspoon capers.

Parmesan Breadsticks

Serves 4

250 g (8 oz) strong white bread flour, plus extra for dusting

½ x 7 g (¼ oz) sachet fast-action dried yeast

½ teaspoon salt

½ tablespoon olive oil

about 150 ml (¼) pint warm water

50 g (2 oz) finely grated Parmesan cheese

- Dust 2 baking sheets with flour. Place the flour, yeast and salt in a bowl and mix together. Stir in the olive oil and 1–2 tablespoons of the measurement water. Mix together with your hand, gradually adding more water, until you have a soft, but not sticky dough.

- Sprinkle over the grated Parmesan and knead the dough well until the cheese is fully incorporated.

- Turn the dough out on to a floured work surface and knead for 5–10 minutes until the dough is smooth and elastic.

- Break into about 16 walnut-sized pieces of dough and roll into long sticks. Place on the prepared baking sheets.

- Bake in a preheated oven, 200°C (400°F), Gas Mark 6, for 4–5 minutes, until golden and crisp. Leave to cool on a wire rack.

1 **Italian Flatbread**
Place 280 g (9 oz) plain flour, 160 g (5 oz) fine semolina, ½ teaspoon salt and 1 tablespoon chopped rosemary in a bowl and mix together. Stir in 1–2 tablespoons of warm water. Mix together with your hand, gradually adding 300 ml (½ pint) warm water until you have a soft, but not sticky dough. Turn out on to a floured work surface and knead for 2–3 minutes. Divide into 8 pieces and roll out to 18–20 cm (7–8 inch) circles. Place the breads on 1 or 2 baking sheets dusted with flour. Bake in a preheated oven, 220°C (425°F), Gas Mark 7, for 2 minutes on each side.

2 **Garlic Bread**
Soften 175 g (6 oz) butter and mix with 4–5 crushed garlic cloves and 4 tablespoons chopped parsley in a bowl. Halve a long baguette and then make 1 cm (½ inch) slits all the way along one of the halves, being careful not to cut all the way through the loaf (save the other half for another use). Spread each side of every slit in the loaf with the garlic butter mixture, pressing the loaf back together when finished. Wrap tightly in foil and bake in the oven at 200°C (400°F) Gas Mark 6 for 15–18 minutes, until golden and crisp.

Baked Mushrooms

Serves 4

8 large portabello mushrooms

3 tablespoons olive oil

8 thyme sprigs

2 tablespoons marsala

100 g (3½ oz) pancetta

50 g (2 oz) chestnuts, chopped

200 g (7 oz) spinach leaves

225 g (7½ oz) mozzarella cheese, grated

salt and pepper

- Place the mushrooms in an ovenproof dish, drizzle with 2 tablespoons of the olive oil, place a thyme sprig in each and pour the marsala around the mushrooms. Bake in a preheated oven, 200 °C (400 °F), Gas Mark 6, for 15–18 minutes.

- Meanwhile, heat the remaining olive oil in a frying pan and cook the pancetta for 4–5 minutes, until browned and just starting to crisp. Stir in the chopped chestnuts and spinach and stir until the spinach has wilted. Season well.

- Remove the mushrooms from the oven, spoon the filling into each one and top with the grated mozzarella. Return to the oven, or cook under a preheated hot grill for 5–6 minutes, until the cheese is melted and golden.

Mushroom and Lentil Soup

Heat 2 tablespoons olive oil in a frying pan and sauté 1 chopped onion and 2 sliced garlic cloves for 2–3 minutes. Add 150 g (5 oz) chopped chestnut mushrooms and cook for 2–3 minutes. Stir in a drained 400 g (13 oz) can green lentils and 1 litre (1¾ pints) vegetable stock and bring to the boil. Simmer for 2–3 minutes and then stir in a small handful of chopped baby spinach leaves, 2 tablespoons chopped parsley and 2 tablespoons grated Parmesan cheese. Serve with crusty bread.

Mushroom Penne

Put 475 g (15 oz) sliced portobello mushrooms, 2 teaspoons wholegrain mustard, 4 crushed garlic cloves, a pinch of dried chilli flakes and 300 ml (½ pint) vegetable stock in a saucepan. Simmer for 10–12 minutes, until the stock has nearly all been absorbed. Meanwhile, cook 400 g (13 oz) penne in a saucepan of boiling water according to the packet instructions, until 'al dente'. Drain the pasta and toss together with the mushrooms, grated rind of 1 lemon, 2 tablespoons chopped parsley and 2 tablespoons grated Parmesan cheese. Serve with a crisp green salad.

30 Peperonata

Serves 4

3 tablespoons olive oil
2 onions, sliced
2 garlic cloves, sliced
2 red peppers, cored, deseeded
  and cut into 1 cm (½ inch) slices
2 yellow peppers, cored, deseeded
  and cut into 1 cm (½ inch) slices
350 g (11½ oz) ripe tomatoes,
  roughly chopped
a small handful of basil leaves,
  shredded

- Heat the olive oil in a medium frying pan and sauté the onion and garlic for 1–2 minutes.

- Add the peppers and cook over a medium heat for a further 10 minutes, then stir in the chopped tomatoes.

- Continue to cook for 15 minutes, until the peppers have started to soften.

- Stir in the basil and serve.

1 Peperonata Salad
Toss together 2 red and 2 yellow cored, deseeded and sliced peppers with 4 sliced tomatoes, a small handful of basil leaves and 50 g (2 oz) baby spinach leaves. Sprinkle with 2 tablespoons olive oil and the juice of ½ lemon and toss again.

2 Quick Peperonata
Heat the olive oil in a medium frying pan and add all the ingredients, except the basil leaves, as above. Cook for 15 minutes, stirring frequently. Serve sprinkled with chopped basil. This is a quicker, crunchier version of the above recipe.

Stuffed Courgettes

Serves 4

4 courgettes
175 g (6 oz) plum tomatoes, chopped
210 g (7 oz) mozzarella cheese, grated
2 tablespoons shredded basil leaves
25 g (1 oz) Parmesan cheese, grated
salt and pepper

- Slice the courgettes in half horizontally and then scoop out the middle of each one, reserving the flesh.

- Place the courgette halves in a roasting tin and bake in a preheated oven, 200°C (400°F), Gas Mark 6, for 10 minutes.

- Meanwhile, chop the reserved courgette flesh and mix in a bowl with the chopped tomatoes, grated mozzarella and basil. Season.

- Remove the courgette halves from the oven and spoon the filling into each one.

- Sprinkle with the grated Parmesan and return to the oven to bake for 15 minutes, until golden.

Courgette and Lemon Salad

Grate 2 large courgettes into a salad bowl and toss together with 1 deseeded and finely chopped red chilli and 5–6 chopped basil leaves. Whisk together 2 tablespoons extra-virgin olive oil, a squeeze of lemon juice and ½ teaspoon honey in a small bowl. Pour the dressing over the courgettes and toss them together to coat with the dressing.

Griddled Courgettes with

Mozzarella Use a vegetable peeler to thinly slice 4 courgettes lengthways. Toss the courgettes in 2 tablespoons olive oil and then cook them on a preheated hot griddle pan for 2–3 minutes on both sides, until griddle marks start to show. Served topped with 210 g (7 oz) torn mozzarella cheese and 6–8 torn basil leaves. Drizzle with a little olive oil, a squeeze of lemon juice and a grinding of pepper.

Sicilian Potato Salad

Serves 4

6–7 potatoes, peeled and
   chopped
1 teaspoon chopped oregano
2 garlic cloves, crushed
1 teaspoon red wine vinegar
3 tablespoons extra-virgin
   olive oil
500 g (1 lb) ripe plum tomatoes,
   roughly chopped
1 red onion, sliced
10–12 black olives, pitted
4 hard-boiled eggs, sliced

· Cook the potatoes in a saucepan of boiling water for
12–15 minutes, until tender. Drain and cool slightly.

· Meanwhile, whisk together the oregano, garlic, red wine
vinegar and olive oil in a small bowl or jar and set aside
until needed.

· Mix together the slightly cooled potatoes, the tomatoes,
red onion, olives and eggs in a large serving dish and
drizzle over the dressing. Leave to stand for 2–3 minutes
before serving.

Sicilian Bean Salad
Make the Sicilian
Potato Salad as above, replacing
the potatoes with a 400 g
(13 oz) can butter beans, rinsed
and drained. Serve immediately.

**Sicilian Tuna and
Potato Salad**
Make the Sicilian Potato Salad
as above. Towards the end of
the potato cooking time, pan-fry
2 x 150 g (5 oz) tuna steaks that
have been seasoned with
pepper, for 4–5 minutes on each
side, depending on how rare you
like your tuna. Leave to rest for
2–3 minutes, then break up and
gently toss into the potato salad.

Black Olive Tapenade on Toasted Ciabatta

Serves 4

3 tablespoons capers
4 anchovy fillets
1 garlic clove, crushed
juice of 1 lemon
250 g (8 oz) black olives, pitted
2 tablespoons chopped parsley
3–4 tablespoons olive oil
1 ciabatta loaf, sliced
salt and pepper

- Place the capers, anchovy fillets, garlic and lemon juice in a food processor or blender and process for about 10 seconds, until you have a rough purée.

- Add the olives, chopped parsley and enough olive oil to make a paste. Blitz again and then season to taste.

- Toast the ciabatta slices on both sides. Spread each slice with tapenade and serve immediately.

---

2 Cod Loin with Black Olive Sauce

Put 200 g (7 oz) roughly chopped pitted black olives, ½ finely diced red chilli, 2 tablespoons chopped basil leaves, 1 crushed garlic clove, the juice of 1 lemon and 2–3 tablespoons olive oil in a bowl and mix to the consistency of a salsa. Heat 2 tablespoons olive oil in a frying pan and cook 4 x 150 g (5 oz) cod fillets for 3–4 minutes on each side, until cooked through. Spoon the olive sauce over the fish and serve with a rocket salad.

3 Asparagus and Tomatoes with Goats' Cheese and Black Olives

Place 450 g (14½ oz) cherry tomatoes in a roasting tin, sprinkle with 2 tablespoons olive oil and season. Add 4 halved garlic cloves and roast in a preheated oven, 200°C (400°F), Gas Mark 6, for 10 minutes. Spoon out some of the tomato juices then add 400 g (13 oz) asparagus spears. Return to the oven and cook for a further 10 minutes. Meanwhile, cook 4 slices of goats' cheese with rind under a preheated hot grill for a few minutes, until slightly golden and soft. Serve the asparagus and tomatoes on 4 warm plates sprinkled with 100 g (3½ oz) pitted black olives and topped with the grilled goats' cheese.

ITA-SOUP-ZOG

Roasted Red Pepper and Goats' Cheese Salad

Serves 4

4 red peppers, halved, cored and deseeded

3 tablespoons extra-virgin olive oil

juice of ½ lemon

1 teaspoon honey

1 teaspoon mustard

1 garlic clove, crushed

75 g (3 oz) pine nuts

150 g (5 oz) goats' cheese

10–12 basil leaves

pepper

- Cook the red peppers, cut side down, under a preheated hot grill for 8–10 minutes, until the skin turns black.

- Meanwhile, whisk together the olive oil, lemon juice, honey, mustard, garlic in a small bowl or jar and season with pepper.

- Place the red pepper in a large bowl, cover with clingfilm and leave until cool enough to handle, then peel away the blackened skin.

- Toast the pine nuts, in a dry frying pan, until they are golden.

- Cut the red peppers into strips and place on a platter. Crumble and scatter over the goats' cheese and the basil leaves and toss together gently.

- Drizzle over the dressing and serve sprinkled with the pine nuts.

Red Pepper, Goats' Cheese and Rocket Salad Core, deseed and thinly slice 4 red peppers, then toss together with 50 g (2 oz) rocket leaves, 8–10 shredded basil leaves and 150 g (5 oz) crumbled goats' cheese in a salad bowl. Drizzle with 2 tablespoons extra-virgin olive oil and 1 tablespoon balsamic vinegar and serve sprinkled with toasted pine nuts.

Red Pepper and Goats' Cheese Bruschetta Make the Red Pepper and Goats's Cheese Salad as above. Cut a large baguette into slices. Drizzle with olive oil and cook under a preheated hot grill on both sides, until toasted and golden. Rub each slice with a garlic clove. Divide the prepared salad mixture between the slices of bread and serve sprinkled with the toasted pine nuts.

Asparagus Frittata

Serves 4

400 g (13 oz) asparagus
2 tablespoons olive oil
6 large eggs
50 g (2 oz) Parmesan cheese, grated
1 tablespoon chopped oregano
salt and pepper

- Break the woody ends off the asparagus and discard. Toss the spears in 1 tablespoon of the olive oil.

- Heat a griddle pan until hot and cook the asparagus for 4–5 minutes, until starting to look a little charred. Cut the asparagus spears into thirds.

- Beat the eggs in a large bowl with the grated Parmesan, oregano and some salt and pepper. Add the asparagus.

- Heat the remaining oil in a flameproof, nonstick frying pan. Pour the mixture into the pan and cook for 8–10 minutes over a low heat, tipping the pan from time to time to allow the runny egg to reach the edges to cook.

- Cook for a further 4–5 minutes under a preheated hot grill, until the top is golden.

- Turn out on to a board, cut into wedges and serve immediately.

Griddled Asparagus

Toss 450 g (14½ oz) trimmed asparagus in 2 tablespoons olive oil. Heat a griddle pan until hot and cook the asparagus for 4–5 minutes, turning once. Serve drizzled with olive oil and sprinkled with Parmesan cheese shavings.

Asparagus Omelettes

Steam 400 g (13 oz) trimmed asparagus for 2–3 minutes, until tender. Meanwhile, whisk together 8 eggs and some salt and pepper in a large bowl with a tiny splash of water. Heat a small frying pan (or omelette pan if you have one) and melt 10 g (⅓ oz) butter. Pour in one-quarter of the egg mixture. Cook for 1 minute, tipping the pan from time to time to allow the runny egg to reach the edges to cook, then leave to cook until the omelette is just set. Sprinkle one-quarter of the asparagus over half of the omelette and fold the other side over the asparagus. Slide on to a warm plate. Repeat with the remaining egg and asparagus to make 4 omelettes.

Spinach and Pecorino Balls with Tomato Sauce

Serves 4

250 g (8 oz) baby spinach leaves
1 egg, beaten
1 garlic clove, crushed
50 g (2 oz) Pecorino cheese, grated
75 g (3 oz) breadcrumbs
1 tablespoon olive oil
2 shallots, diced
400 g (13 oz) can chopped tomatoes
50 ml (2 fl oz) red wine
2 tablespoons shredded basil leaves
vegetable oil, for frying
salt and pepper
4 tablespoons grated Parmesan cheese, to serve

- Steam the spinach for 1–2 minutes, until wilted. Squeeze out any excess moisture and roughly chop.

- Mix the spinach with the egg, garlic, Pecorino, breadcrumbs and some salt and pepper in a bowl.

- Roll the mixture into walnut-sized balls and chill for 15 minutes.

- Meanwhile, make the tomato sauce. Heat the olive oil in a saucepan and sauté the shallots for 2–3 minutes. Pour in the chopped tomatoes and red wine and add the basil. Simmer for 8–10 minutes.

- Heat vegetable oil in a deep frying pan until it is 180–190°C (350–375°F), or until a cube of bread browns in 30 seconds when dropped into the oil.

- Working in batches, cook the spinach balls for 3–4 minutes, until they are golden. Remover with a slotted spoon and drain on kitchen paper.

- Serve with the tomato sauce and a good sprinkling of grated Parmesan.

---

10 **Spinach and Pecorino Salad**

Whisk together 3 tablespoons extra-virgin olive oil, 1 tablespoon balsamic vinegar, 1 teaspoon Dijon mustard and ½ teaspoon honey. Toss together 175 g (6 oz) baby spinach leaves, 3 tablespoons toasted pine nuts, 2 tablespoons sultanas and 1 cored, deseeded and thinly sliced red pepper. Toss in the dressing along with 4 tablespoons Pecorino shavings.

20 **Spinach and Pecorino Pasta**

Cook 400 g (13 oz) spiral pasta shapes in a saucepan of boiling water according to the packet instructions, until 'al dente'. Meanwhile, heat 1 tablespoon olive oil in a frying pan and sauté 2 diced shallots for 3–4 minutes. Stir in 150 g (5 oz) ricotta cheese, 12 quartered cherry tomatoes and 100 g (3½ oz) baby spinach leaves and mix well. Drain the pasta and stir into the sauce. Serve sprinkled with 3 tablespoons grated Pecorino cheese.

Layered Potatoes and Mushrooms

Serves 4

butter, for greasing

600 g (1¼ lb) potatoes,
  peeled and thinly sliced

300 g (10 oz) chestnut or porcini
  mushrooms, thinly sliced

1 large onion, thinly sliced

125 ml (4 fl oz) olive oil

3 tablespoons chopped parsley

50 g (2 oz) breadcrumbs

50 g (2 oz) Parmesan cheese,
  grated

salt and pepper

- Grease an ovenproof dish or roasting tin. Blanch the potatoes in a saucepan of boiling water for 2–3 minutes and then drain.

- Layer the potatoes, mushrooms and onion in the greased ovenproof dish, drizzling each layer with olive oil and sprinkling with chopped parsley.

- Season well and sprinkle over the breadcrumbs and Parmesan. Bake in a preheated oven, 200°C (400°F), Gas Mark 6, for 22 minutes, until the potato is completely cooked and the topping is golden.

---

1 Garlicky Mushrooms

with Mashed Potatoes Heat 3 tablespoons olive oil and 25 g (1 oz) butter in a frying pan and sauté 3 crushed garlic cloves for 1–2 minutes. Add 300 g (10 oz) sliced chestnut mushrooms and cook for 4–5 minutes. Meanwhile, heat 600 g (1¼ lb) shop-bought ready-made mashed potatoes according to the packet instructions. Stir 1 tablespoon chopped parsley into the mushrooms and serve spooned over the mash. Serve drizzled with 1 tablespoon olive oil.

2 Bean, Potato and Mushroom Salad

Cook 250 g (8 oz) new potatoes in a saucepan of boiling water for about 12–15 minutes, until tender. Add 200 g (7 oz) green beans for the last 3 minutes of cooking. Drain and refresh under cold running water, put in a serving bowl and toss in 3 tablespoons olive oil. Add 1 sliced red onion, 1 tablespoon capers and 125 g (4 oz) halved cherry tomatoes. Heat 2 tablespoons olive oil in a frying pan and cook 125 g (4 oz) diced pancetta and 50 g (2 oz) diced chestnut mushrooms, until the pancetta is crisp. Sprinkle over the salad to serve.

Roasted Tomato Soup

Serves 4

1 kg (2 lb) ripe tomatoes, halved
4 garlic cloves, unpeeled
2 tablespoons olive oil
1 onion, chopped
1 carrot, chopped
1 celery stick, sliced
1 red pepper, cored, deseeded and chopped
700 ml (1 pint 3 fl oz) hot vegetable stock
salt and pepper
4 tablespoons grated Parmesan cheese, to serve

- Place the tomato halves and garlic cloves in a roasting tin. Sprinkle with 1 tablespoon of the olive oil and some pepper and roast in a preheated oven, 200°C (400°F), Gas Mark 6, for 20 minutes.

- After 10 minutes, heat the remaining olive oil in a saucepan and sauté the onion, carrot, celery and red pepper over a low heat for 10 minutes.

- When the tomatoes are cooked, remove the garlic cloves in their skins and squeeze the garlic flesh into the pan with the sautéed vegetables.

- Pour in the roast tomatoes and all the juices along with the stock. Using a hand blender, or in a food processor or blender, blend the soup until smooth. Season to taste.

- Reheat if necessary, then serve sprinkled with the Parmesan.

Quick Tomato Toasts

Toast 4 slices of bread on both sides, then rub each slice with a garlic clove and sprinkle with shredded basil leaves. Slice 4 tomatoes and place the tomato slices on top of the basil. Sprinkle with 125 g (4 oz) grated mozzarella cheese and cook under a preheated hot grill, until the cheese is bubbling and golden.

Quick Tomato Soup

Heat 2 tablespoons olive oil in a saucepan and sauté 1 chopped onion, 1 chopped carrot, 1 celery stick and 700 g (1½ lb) chopped tomatoes for 5 minutes. Pour in a 400 g (13 oz) can chopped tomatoes and 900 ml (1½ pints) hot vegetable stock. Simmer for 10 minutes, remove from the heat and add a small handful of basil leaves. Using a hand blender, or in a food processor or blender, blend the soup until smooth. Season to taste and serve with an extra drizzle of olive oil.

Baked Ricotta

Serves 4

475 g (15 oz) ricotta cheese

grated rind of 1 lemon

4 eggs, beaten

40 g (1¾ oz) Parmesan cheese, grated

1 teaspoon finely chopped thyme leaves

625 g (1 lb 6 oz) baby spinach leaves

4 ripe tomatoes, chopped

pepper

2 teaspoons extra-virgin olive oil, to serve

- Beat together the ricotta, lemon rind, eggs, Parmesan and thyme in a bowl and season with pepper. Spoon into 4 ramekin dishes.

- Bake in a preheated oven, 190°C (375°F), Gas Mark 5, for 20–22 minutes, until risen and lightly golden.

- Meanwhile, steam the spinach for 1–2 minutes, until wilted, then divide between 4 plates.

- Leave the baked ricotta to cool for 1–2 minutes. Run a knife around the outside and then turn each one out on to a bed of steamed spinach.

- Sprinkle over the chopped tomatoes and serve drizzled with the olive oil.

---

1 **Quick Ricotta Dip**
Stir 2 tablespoons shop-bought ready-made pesto and 2 tablespoons toasted pine nuts into 300 g (10 oz) ricotta cheese in a bowl. Core and deseed 2 red and 2 yellow peppers, slice them into thin strips and serve with the dip.

2 **Ricotta-Stuffed Pasta Shells**
Cook 400 g (13 oz) conchiglioni in a saucepan of boiling water for 10–12 minutes, until 'al dente'. Meanwhile, chop 3 deseeded tomatoes and mix with 500 g (1 lb) ricotta cheese and 2 tablespoons shredded basil.

Place a spoonful of the ricotta mixture into each pasta shell and lay them in a greased ovenproof dish. Drizzle with 2 tablespoons olive oil and sprinkle with 2 tablespoons grated Parmesan cheese. Place under a preheated hot grill for 2–3 minutes. Serve with a crisp, green salad.

Broad Beans with Anchovies and Tomatoes

Serves 4

1.3 kg (2½ lb) (fresh or frozen) broad beans

3 tablespoons olive oil

450 g (14½ oz) cherry tomatoes, halved

6 spring onions, sliced

2 garlic cloves, finely sliced

6 anchovy fillets, chopped

1 tablespoon shredded basil leaves

1 tablespoon chopped parsley

50 g (2 oz) rocket leaves

2 tablespoons Parmesan cheese shavings, to serve

- Blanch the broad beans in a saucepan of boiling water for 1 minute and then refresh under cold water. Drain and peel off the outer skins.

- Heat the olive oil in a frying pan and cook the tomatoes over a medium heat for 4–5 minutes.

- Add the spring onions and garlic and cook for a further 1–2 minutes, then add the broad beans.

- Stir in the anchovies and herbs and cook for 1–2 minutes.

- Spoon into a large serving bowl, toss with the rocket leaves and serve topped with Parmesan shavings.

Butter Bean and Anchovy Mash

Heat 2 x 400 g (13 oz) cans butter beans, rinsed and drained in a saucepan of boiling water for 2–3 minutes and then drain. Whizz together ½ chopped red chilli and 4 anchovy fillets in a food processor or blender. Pour in the warmed butter beans and process until roughly chopped. Stir in a small handful of chopped parsley, the juice of ½ lemon and 2–3 tablespoons olive oil, to make a chunky butter bean mash. Great served with grilled lamb.

Roasted Peppers with Tomatoes and Anchovies

Place 4 halved, cored and deseeded peppers, cut sides up, in a roasting tin. Halve 8 tomatoes and divide between the peppers. Top each one with 1–2 anchovy fillets, a few slices of garlic and a few rosemary sprigs. Drizzle with 2–3 tablespoons olive oil, season with pepper and bake in a preheated oven, 200°C (400°F), Gas Mark 6, for 22–25 minutes.

ITA-SOUP-DUP

Mozzarella and Spinach Stuffed Pancakes

Serves 4

125 g (4 oz) plain flour
a pinch of salt
2 eggs
200 ml (7 fl oz) milk mixed with
  75 ml (3 fl oz) water
50 g (2 oz) butter, melted
200 g (7 oz) baby spinach leaves
4 tomatoes, sliced
400 g (13 oz) mozzarella cheese,
  sliced
2 tablespoons grated Parmesan
  cheese

- To make the batter, sift the flour and salt into a large bowl. Make a well in the centre and break the eggs into it. Whisk the eggs into the flour and then gradually add a small amount of the milk and water, still whisking.

- Whisk half the melted butter into the pancake batter and use the remainder to grease a frying pan. Rub the pan with kitchen paper to take off any excess.

- Pour about 2 tablespoons of the batter into the pan and swirl around to completely coat the base. After about 1 minute check that the pancake is cooked underneath and then flip it over to cook the other side for just a few seconds.

- Sprinkle half the pancake with some spinach leaves, sliced tomatoes and sliced mozzarella. Fold the other half of the pancake over the filled side and press lightly. Transfer the filled pancake to an ovenproof dish and keep warm.

- Repeat with the remaining ingredients. Sprinkle the pancakes with the grated Parmesan and briefly cook under a preheated hot grill until golden. Serve immediately.

---

10 Mozzarella and Spinach Salad

Layer 100 g (3½ oz) spinach leaves with 400 g (13 oz) sliced mozzarella cheese, 2 thinly sliced beefsteak tomatoes and 10–12 basil leaves on a large platter. Sprinkle with 2 teaspoons chopped oregano and 2 tablespoons toasted pine nuts and drizzle with 3 tablespoons extra-virgin olive oil and 1 tablespoon balsamic vinegar.

20 Mozzarella and Spinach Pizza

Place 2 large ready-made pizza bases on 2 baking sheets and spread with 500 g (1 lb) passata. Heat 2 tablespoons olive oil in a large frying pan and sauté 2 sliced garlic cloves and 1 sliced red onion for 2–3 minutes, then stir in 500 g (1 lb) baby spinach leaves. Continue to stir until the spinach has completely wilted. Spread the wilted spinach over the pizza bases, then sprinkle with 250 g (8 oz) grated mozzarella cheese, 1 tablespoon chopped basil leaves and some pepper. Bake in a preheated oven, 200°C (400°F), Gas Mark 6, for 12–15 minutes, until the cheese is melted and golden.

 # Italian Vegetable Kebabs

Serves 4

2 red peppers, cored, deseeded and chopped

1 yellow pepper, cored, deseeded and chopped

2 courgettes, cut into thick slices

1 large red onion, cut into wedges

2 tablespoons olive oil

2 tablespoons lemon juice

2 tablespoons torn basil leaves

salt and pepper

- Place the chopped vegetables in a large bowl and toss in the olive oil, lemon juice, basil and salt and pepper.

- Thread the vegetables on to metal skewers and grill or barbecue over a medium heat for 10–12 minutes, turning occasionally, until cooked. Serve immediately.

Griddled Vegetables

Thickly slice 3 courgettes lengthways, and core, deseed and thickly sliced 2 red and 2 yellow peppers. Heat a griddle pan until hot and cook the vegetables for about 4–5 minutes, until charred and starting to soften. Place on a platter and sprinkle with 3 tablespoons Parmesan cheese shavings and 2 tablespoons shredded basil leaves. Drizzle with Italian salad dressing to serve.

 ### Italian Vegetable Kebabs with Herb

Pasta Cook 300 g (10 oz) tagliatelle according to the packet instructions, until 'al dente'. When cooked, drain the pasta and toss with 2 tablespoons torn basil leaves and 2 tablespoons olive oil. Meanwhile, heat 1 tablespoon olive oil in a frying pan and cook 1 diced red chilli and 1 diced garlic clove for 1 minute, then add 100 g (3½ oz) mushrooms, 1 red pepper, cored, deseeded and cut into chunks, and 1 sliced courgette. Cook for 2–3 minutes. Thread the vegetables on to soaked wooden skewers with 125 g (4 oz) chopped haloumi cheese and 3 thickly sliced spring onions. Cook under a preheated hot grill for 2–3 minutes to heat through. Serve the kebabs on a bed of the herbed pasta.

 # Wild Mushroom Tart

Serves 4

375 g (12 oz) ready-rolled
  shortcrust pastry
10 g (⅓ oz) dried porcini
2 tablespoons olive oil
1 red onion, sliced
350 g (11½ oz) mushrooms
  (include a variety of wild
  and chestnut)
2 eggs, beaten
100 g (3½ oz) mascarpone
  cheese
1 teaspoon thyme leaves
2 teaspoons wholegrain mustard
40 g (1¾ oz) Parmesan cheese,
  grated
pepper

- Use the pastry to line a 23 cm (9 inch) flan tin. Chill for 5 minutes.

- Soak the porcini in a bowl with enough boiling water to just cover them.

- Heat the olive oil in a frying pan and cook the onion and mushrooms for 5 minutes, stirring frequently.

- Beat together the eggs, mascarpone and thyme leaves in a bowl and season with pepper.

- Drain and chop the porcini and add to the egg, along with the mushrooms from the frying pan. Mix well.

- Spread the mustard over the base of the pastry. Pour over the mushroom mixture and level with the back of a spoon.

- Sprinkle with the grated Parmesan and bake in a preheated oven, 200°C (400°F), Gas Mark 6, for 20 minutes until golden. Slice into generous pieces and serve hot or cold.

1 Mushroom and Taleggio

Bruschetta Heat 2 tablespoons olive oil in a frying pan and sauté 100 g (3½ oz) wild mushrooms with 1 crushed garlic clove for 4–5 minutes. Stir in 1 tablespoon chopped parsley. Toast 8 slices of large baguette on both sides. Top each slice of bread with the mushroom mixture and then a slice of taleggio cheese. Cook under a preheated hot grill for 1–2 minutes, until the cheese is bubbling. Serve warm.

2 Wild Mushroom Ragout with

Polenta Heat 2 tablespoons olive oil in a frying pan and cook 350 g (11½ oz) mixed wild mushrooms with 2 crushed garlic cloves for 2–3 minutes. Stir in 1 tablespoon chopped tarragon, 1 tablespoon chopped thyme leaves and a drizzle of truffle oil (optional). Bring 800 ml (1¼ pints) water to the boil and add 200 g (7 oz) instant polenta. Cook, stirring constantly, for 1 minute, then stir in 25 g (1 oz)

butter and some salt and pepper. Spread the polenta in the base of an ovenproof dish and pour over the mushroom mixture. Dot with 200 g (7 oz) chopped taleggio cheese and cook under a preheated hot grill, until the cheese is melted and golden.

Tomato, Basil and Mozzarella Salad

Serves 4

3 tablespoons extra-virgin olive oil

juice of ½ lemon

1 teaspoon honey

1 teaspoon mustard

1 garlic clove, crushed

875 g (1¾ lb) ripe tomatoes

420 g (13¾ oz) mozzarella cheese, sliced

10–12 basil leaves, shredded

pepper

- Whisk together the olive oil, lemon juice, honey, mustard, garlic and some pepper in a bowl.

- Place the tomatoes in a large bowl and pour over boiling water. Leave to stand for 30 seconds, then drain and refresh under cold water. Peel off the skins and slice the tomatoes.

- Layer the tomatoes with slices of mozzarella and torn basil leaves on plates or a large serving bowl.

- Drizzle over the dressing and leave to stand for 5 minutes before serving.

---

10 Speedy Tomato and Mozzarella Salad Thinly slice 875 g (1¾ lb) ripe plum tomatoes and layer on a platter with 420 g (13¾ oz) sliced mozzarella cheese and 10–12 basil leaves. Drizzle with olive oil and balsamic vinegar and serve.

30 Tomato and Mozzarella Tart Roll 300 g (10 oz) shop-bought chilled puff pastry out on a lightly floured work surface to 25 cm (10 inches) square. Place on a baking sheet and score a square about 2.5 cm (1 inch) in from the edge. Bake in a preheated oven, 200°C (400°F), Gas Mark 6, for 10 minutes, until golden. Slice 600 g (1¼ lb) ripe tomatoes and 210 g (7 oz) mozzarella cheese and place these, slightly overlapping, in the centre square, letting the edge remain risen. Top with 10–12 basil leaves and sprinkle with 2 tablespoons pine nuts. Bake for a further 10–12 minutes, until the cheese is melted and the pastry is golden. Serve with 60 g (2¼ oz) rocket leaves in 2 tablespoons olive oil and 1 tablespoon balsamic vinegar.

Pear, Walnut and Gorgonzola Salad

Serves 4

3 tablespoons extra-virgin
   olive oil
1 teaspoon Dijon mustard
1 tablespoon white wine vinegar
1 teaspoon caster sugar
40 g (1¾ oz) walnut pieces
1 radicchio, leaves separated
50 g (2 oz) rocket leaves
1 romaine heart, leaves separated
   and torn
2 pears, cored and sliced
175 g (6 oz) Gorgonzola cheese,
   crumbled

- Whisk together the olive oil, mustard, vinegar and sugar in a small bowl or measuring jug.

- Toast the walnut pieces in a dry frying pan, until golden, to help bring out their flavour.

- Toss together the radicchio, rocket and romaine heart leaves in a bowl. Divide the leaves between 4 plates and sprinkle with the slices of pear, crumbled Gorgonzola and the walnuts.

- Pour over the dressing and serve.

2 Gorgonzola with Warm Marsala

Pears Place 4 x 100 g (3½ oz) slices of Gorgonzola cheese in a serving dish. Core and cut 2 pears into eighths. Heat 1 tablespoon olive oil in a frying pan and cook the pears for 3–4 minutes on each side. Whisk together 2 tablespoons honey and 2 tablespoons marsala then pour into the pan, letting it simmer and thicken for a few minutes. Using a slotted spoon, remove the pears and place them on top of the Gorgonzola. Fry 60 g (2¼ oz) walnut halves in the remaining syrup in the pan. Pour the syrup and walnuts over the pears and Gorgonzola to serve.

3 Pear, Walnut and Gorgonzola Pizza

Heat 1 tablespoon olive oil in a frying pan and sauté 1 large sliced red onion for about 4–5 minutes, until softened. Add 2 cored and sliced pears. Stir in 2 tablespoons balsamic vinegar and some pepper and cook until the onions start to caramelize. Spread 4 ready-made pizza bases with 2 tablespoons passata, then divide the pear mixture between the bases. Top each one with 200 g (7 oz) crumbled Gorgonzola cheese and 60 g (2¼ oz) walnuts. Bake in a preheated oven, 200°C (400°F), Gas Mark 6, for 10–12 minutes.

Borlotti Bean and Roasted Red Pepper Bruschetta

Serves 4

1 large baguette, cut into 8 slices

3 tablespoons olive oil

1 garlic clove

400 g (13 oz) can borlotti beans, rinsed and drained

3 spring onions, sliced

100 g (3½ oz) roasted red peppers from a jar, drained and finely sliced

6 basil leaves, thinly shredded

salt and pepper

- Place the slices of baguette on a baking sheet and drizzle with 2 tablespoons of the olive oil. Cook under a preheated hot grill for 2–3 minutes on each side, until toasted and golden.

- Rub each slice of toast with the garlic clove.

- Place the drained borlotti beans and spring onions in a bowl and lightly crush together with a fork.

- Stir in the red pepper, basil, remaining olive oil and some salt and pepper.

- Spoon the bean mixture on to the toasted baguette slices and serve immediately.

Quick Bean Salad

In a large serving bowl, mix together a 400 g (13 oz) can borlotti beans, rinsed and drained, 3 sliced spring onions, 100 g (3½ oz) drained and chopped roasted red peppers from a jar, 3 chopped tomatoes, 4–5 shredded basil leaves, 2 tablespoons olive oil and 1 tablespoon balsamic vinegar.

Bean and Roasted Red Pepper Salad

Halve, core and deseed 4 red peppers and cook, cut-side down, under a preheated hot grill, until the skin turns black. Place in a large bowl, cover with clingfilm and leave until they are cool enough to handle. Meanwhile, whisk together 3 tablespoons extra-virgin olive oil, the juice of ½ lemon, 1 teaspoon Dijon mustard and ½ teaspoon sugar. Toss together 1 torn romaine lettuce, 1 small red onion, peeled and thinly sliced, 150 g (5 oz) halved cherry tomatoes, 2 tablespoons roughly chopped parsley and a 400 g (13 oz) can borlotti beans, rinsed and drained. When the peppers are cool enough to handle, peel away the blackened skin and cut into strips. Toss these with the other salad ingredients. Cook 4 slices of goats' cheese with rind under a hot grill for 3–4 minutes, until slightly golden and soft. Divide the salad between 4 plates or shallow bowls and top each one with a slice of grilled goats' cheese. Drizzle with the dressing and serve sprinkled with 1 tablespoon chopped oregano leaves.

Arancini

Serves 4

700 g (1½ lb) cold spinach risotto, either leftover or ready-cooked shop-bought

100 g (3½ oz) mozzarella cheese, cut into cubes

2 eggs, beaten

150 g (5 oz) fresh breadcrumbs

750–900 ml (1¼–1½ pints) groundnut oil

rocket leaves, to serve

- Using wet hands, take a small handful of cold risotto and roll into a ball. Press a cube of mozzarella into the middle of the ball and seal by squeezing the rice around it. Repeat with the remaining risotto and mozzarella to make about 12 balls.

- Place the beaten egg in one shallow bowl and the breadcrumbs in another. Dip each ball into the egg first and then the breadcrumbs to coat completely.

- Pour the groundnut oil into a deep-fat fryer or large saucepan, and heat until it is 180–190°C (350–375°F), or until a cube of bread browns in 30 seconds when dropped into the oil. Working in batches, cook the arancini for 3–4 minutes, until golden. Remove with a slotted spoon and drain on kitchen paper.

- Serve hot with rocket leaves.

---

1 **Rice Salad**

Gently toss together 400 g (13 oz) shop-bought ready-cooked long grain rice, 250 g (8 oz) canned asparagus tips, 1 cored, deseeded and chopped red pepper, 2 tablespoons chopped sun-dried tomatoes, the grated rind and juice of 1 lemon, 2 tablespoons extra-virgin olive oil, 250 g (8 oz) halved mini mozzarellas and a large handful of shredded basil leaves. Season well and serve.

3 **Rice with Chicken**

Heat 2 tablespoons olive oil in a saucepan and brown 2 boneless, skinless chicken breasts, sliced into strips, for 3–4 minutes. Add 2 thickly sliced red onions, 3 sliced garlic cloves and 3 cored, deseeded and thickly sliced red peppers and cook for a further 4–5 minutes. Stir in 200 g (7 oz) long-grain rice, a 400 g (13 oz) can chopped tomatoes and 450 ml (¾ pint) chicken stock. Bring to the boil and then transfer to and ovenproof dish. Bake in a preheated oven, 200°C (400°F), Gas Mark 6, for 15–18 minutes, until the stock is absorbed and the rice and chicken are cooked. Serve sprinkled with 2 tablespoons grated Parmesan cheese.

Savoy Cabbage and Parmesan Soup

Serves 4

4 tablespoons olive oil
1 onion, chopped
2 garlic cloves, crushed
½ teaspoon fennel seeds
1 savoy cabbage
1 potato, diced
1 litre (1¾ pints) vegetable stock
75 g (3 oz) grated Parmesan
  cheese, plus extra 1 tablespoon
  to serve
salt and pepper
crusty bread, to serve

- Heat 2 tablespoons of the olive oil in a saucepan and sauté the onion, garlic and fennel seeds for 3–4 minutes.

- Shred 4 leaves of the cabbage and reserve. Finely shred the remaining cabbage, add to the pan with the diced potato and cook for 3–4 minutes, then pour in the stock.

- Simmer for 10 minutes, until the potato is tender. Stir in the grated Parmesan.

- Using a hand blender, or in a food processor or blender, blend the soup until smooth. Season to taste.

- Heat the remaining olive oil and stir-fry the reserved cabbage. Top each bowl of soup with the fried cabbage.

- Serve sprinkled with extra grated Parmesan, and slices of crusty bread on the side.

1 Coleslaw with Italian Dressing

Whisk together 3 tablespoons extra-virgin olive oil, 1 tablespoon white wine vinegar, 1 tablespoon chopped parsley, ½ tablespoon lemon juice, 1 crushed garlic clove, ½ teaspoon dried basil and a pinch of dried oregano. In a large bowl, shred ½ white cabbage, 2 carrots and ½ onion and mix with the dressing to serve.

2 Rice with Savoy Cabbage

Heat 3 tablespoons olive oil in a frying pan and sauté 1 chopped onion for 2–3 minutes. Stir in 450 g (14½ oz) finely shredded savoy cabbage and cook, stirring, until wilted. Stir in 250 g (8 oz) Arborio rice and 1 litre (1¾ pints) beef stock. Bring to the boil and simmer for 15–16 minutes, until the rice is 'al dente'. Stir in 25 g (1 oz) butter and 40 g (1¾ oz) grated Parmesan, season and serve.

ITA-SOUP-SEW

30 Aubergine Melts

Serves 4

2 aubergines, halved lengthways
4 tablespoons olive oil
4 tomatoes, sliced
200 g (7 oz) mozzarella cheese, sliced
a small handful of basil leaves
2 tablespoons toasted pine nuts
pepper
crisp green salad, to serve

- Place the aubergine halves on a baking sheet, drizzle with the olive oil and bake in a preheated oven, 200°C (400°F), Gas Mark 6 for 20 minutes until softened.

- Remove the aubergine from the oven, arrange the slices of tomato and mozzarella on top and bake for a further 5 minutes, until the cheese has melted.

- Scatter with basil leaves and pine nuts, season with pepper and serve with a crisp green salad.

---

10 **Aubergine Dip and Caramelized Onion Bruschetta** Heat 1 tablespoon olive oil in a frying pan and cook 1 sliced onion over a low heat for 6 minutes, stirring occasionally, until the onion starts to caramelize. Sprinkle in ½ teaspoon sugar and 1 teaspoon balsamic vinegar and cook for another minute. Toast 8 slices of ciabatta on both sides, then spread with ready-made aubergine dip. Spoon over the caramelized onions to serve.

 20 **Aubergine and Goats' Cheese Pasta** Cook 400 g (13 oz) pasta shapes of your choice in a saucepan of boiling water according to the packet instructions, until 'al dente'. Meanwhile, heat 1 tablespoon olive oil in a frying pan and fry 1 chopped onion and 2 sliced garlic cloves for 3–4 minutes. Add 1 chopped aubergine and cook for a further 4–5 minutes. Pour in a 400 g (13 oz) can chopped tomatoes and simmer for 3–4 minutes. Drain the pasta and stir into the sauce with 100 g (3½ oz) crumbled goats' cheese and a small handful of torn basil leaves and mix well.

30 Baked Fennel and Gorgonzola

Serves 4

4 fennel bulbs
3 tablespoons olive oil
200 g (7 oz) Gorgonzola cheese
pepper

- Trim the fennel bulbs and slice vertically.

- Heat the oil in a frying pan and sauté the fennel for 2–3 minutes, then transfer to an ovenproof dish.

- Break the Gorgonzola into chunks and scatter these over the fennel.

- Bake in a preheated oven, 200°C (400°F), Gas Mark 6, for 25 minutes, until the fennel is tender and has turned slightly golden at the edges.

10 Quick Fennel Coleslaw

Mix together 2 fennel bulbs, 2 large carrots, 1 small onion, all finely sliced, with ½ tablespoon chopped parsley, 1 tablespoon mayonnaise and the juice of ½ lemon.

20 Gorgonzola Croûtons with Fennel and Orange Salad

Peel and segment 2 oranges over a bowl to catch the juice. Whisk the orange juice with 3 tablespoons extra-virgin olive oil, 2 teaspoons honey and 1 teaspoon wholegrain mustard. Toast 3 tablespoons pumpkin seeds in a dry frying pan until golden. Toss together the orange segments, 2 finely sliced fennel bulbs, 50 g (2 oz) watercress and the dressing. For the croûtons, cut a baguette into 8 slices. Toast each slice on one side under a preheated hot grill, then turn over and top with 175 g (6 oz) Gorgonzola cheese. Cook until the cheese is bubbling and golden. Divide the salad between 4 plates and top each one with 2 Gorgonzola croûtons. Sprinkle with the toasted pumpkin seeds before serving.

ITA-SOUP-QYD

Wild Mushroom Crostini

Serves 4

2 thin baguettes
4 tablespoons olive oil
2 garlic cloves, 1 whole, 1 crushed
1 shallot, diced
125 g (4 oz) mixed wild
   mushrooms, chopped
1 tablespoon chopped parsley
pepper

- Cut the baguettes into slices diagonally, about 2.5 cm (1 inch) thick. Place the slices on a baking sheet and brush with 2 tablespoons of the olive oil.

- Bake in a preheated oven, 200°C (400°F), Gas Mark 6, for 4–5 minutes, until golden brown. Rub each slice with the whole garlic clove and keep the slices warm.

- Heat the remaining oil in a frying pan and sauté the shallot and crushed garlic for 3–4 minutes, then add the mushrooms and cook them until they have released all of their juices. Stir in the chopped parsley and season with pepper.

- Spoon the mushroom mixture on to the crostini and serve.

Wild Mushroom Omelette

Heat 1 tablespoon olive oil and 20 g (¾ oz) butter in an omelette pan and sauté ½ small sliced onion for 1–2 minutes. Stir in 125 g (4 oz) wild mushrooms and cook for 2–3 minutes. Pour in 6 beaten eggs with ½ tablespoon chopped tarragon, tipping the pan from time to time to allow the runny egg to reach the edges to cook. When almost cooked, carefully fold over one side of the omelette and slide on to a warm plate. Divide into 2 to serve. Repeat with the same ingredients to make another omelette to be divided into 2. Serve with a green salad.

Asparagus and Wild Mushroom

Pasta Cook 400 g (13 oz) pasta in a saucepan of boiling water according to the packet instructions, until 'al dente'. Meanwhile, heat 1 tablespoon olive oil in a frying pan and sauté 400 g (13 oz) trimmed and halved asparagus for 3–4 minutes. Pour in 4 tablespoons vegetable stock, ½ teaspoon dried chilli flakes and 200 g (7 oz) wild mushrooms (if wild not available, normal field mushrooms can be used). Cook for 4–5 minutes. Drain the pasta and gently toss in the asparagus mixture. Serve sprinkled with 2 tablespoons grated Parmesan cheese.

Cream of Pumpkin and Apple Soup

Serves 4

2 tablespoons olive oil
1 onion, chopped
600 g (1 ⅛ lb) pumpkin flesh,
  cut into chunks
1 Bramley apple, peeled, cored
  and chopped
2 tomatoes, skinned and chopped
900 ml (1½ pints) vegetable
  stock
100 ml (3½ fl oz) double cream
1 tablespoon finely chopped
  parsley
salt and pepper

- Place the tomatoes in a large bowl and pour over boiling water. Leave to stand for 30 seconds, then drain and refresh under cold water. Peel off the skins and chop the tomatoes.

- Heat the olive oil in a large saucepan and sauté the onion for 3–4 minutes.

- Add the pumpkin and stir to coat with the onions. Stir in the apple and the chopped tomatoes.

- Pour in the stock, bring to the boil and then simmer, covered, for 20 minutes, until the pumpkin is tender.

- Leave the soup to cool a little before pouring in the cream. Using a hand blender, or in a food processor or blender, blend the soup until smooth.

- Gently reheat if necessary, season and serve immediately, sprinkling in the chopped parsley.

Pumpkin Hummus
Blend together
200 g (7 oz) canned pumpkin purée, 3 tablespoons tahini, 1–2 crushed garlic cloves, a 400 g (13 oz) can chickpeas, rinsed and drained, 1 tablespoon lemon juice and ½ teaspoon ground cumin in a food processor or blender. Gradually add olive oil until you have the consistency you like. Add salt and pepper to taste and serve with vegetable crudités.

Pumpkin and Chickpea Salad
Cut 1 kg (2 lb) pumpkin flesh into small dice. Toss with 1 crushed garlic clove, ½ teaspoon ground cumin and 2 tablespoons olive oil and roast in a preheated oven, 200 °C (400 °F), Gas Mark 6, for 15 minutes. Mix the roasted pumpkin with a 400 g (13 oz) can chickpeas, rinsed and drained, 1 small diced red onion, 150 g (5 oz) crumbled feta cheese, 50 g (2 oz) sun-dried tomatoes and 50 g (2 oz) rocket leaves. Serve dressed with Italian salad dressing.

Grilled Radicchio with Pancetta

Serves 4

2 tablespoons olive oil
½ tablespoon balsamic vinegar
3 garlic cloves, crushed
1 tablespoon chopped rosemary
2 radicchio heads, cut into
    quarters through the core end
8 pancetta slices
pepper
Pecorino cheese shavings, to
    serve

- Whisk together the olive oil, vinegar, garlic and rosemary in a large non-metallic bowl and season with pepper. Add the radicchio and toss to coat. Leave to stand for 10 minutes.

- Wrap each quarter of radicchio with a slice of pancetta.

- Cook the radicchio under a preheated hot grill or on a hot barbecue grill for 5–6 minutes, until the edges are crisp and slightly charred, turning occasionally.

- Serve on a platter drizzled with the remaining marinade and sprinkled with Pecorino shavings.

Radicchio Slaw

Cook 50 g (2 oz) diced pancetta under a preheated hot grill until crisp. Meanwhile, mix together 1 thinly sliced radicchio head, 2 carrots and 1 fennel bulb, both cut into matchsticks, 2 tablespoons mayonnaise, the juice of ½ lemon and some salt and pepper. Sprinkle with the crisp pancetta to serve.

Radicchio Risotto

Heat 2 tablespoons olive oil in a saucepan and sauté 2 finely chopped onions with 50 g (2 oz) diced pancetta for 3–5 minutes. Add 1 shredded radicchio head and cook for 2–3 minutes. Stir in 300 g (10 oz) Arborio rice, until the edges of the grains look translucent. Pour in 200 ml (7 fl oz) white wine and cook for 1–2 minutes, until it is all absorbed. Add a ladle from 750 ml (1¼ pints) hot chicken stock and stir continuously, until it has all been absorbed. Repeat with the remaining hot stock, adding a ladle at a time, until the rice is 'al dente'. Remove from the heat and stir in 25 g (1 oz) butter and 25 g (1 oz) grated Parmesan cheese. Serve sprinkled with an extra 2–3 tablespoons grated Parmesan.

Cheese-Stuffed Onions

Serves 4

4 large onions, peeled
150 g (5 oz) spinach leaves
100 g (3½ oz) ricotta cheese
1 egg yolk
1 teaspoon chopped thyme leaves
25 g (1 oz) Fontina cheese
40 g (1¾ oz) Parmesan cheese,
   grated
25 g (1 oz) butter

To serve

50 g (2 oz) rocket leaves
3 tablespoons balsamic syrup

- Blanch the onions in boiling water for 5 minutes. Drain and leave to cool for 5 minutes.

- Meanwhile, heat 1 tablespoon olive oil in a large saucepan, cook the spinach until wilted and then roughly chop. Place in a bowl with the ricotta, egg yolk, thyme, Fontina and 20 g (¾ oz) of the grated Parmesan.

- Slice off the top of each onion and remove the middle sections with a fork.

- Spoon the cheese mixture into the onions and place them in a roasting tin. Sprinkle over the remaining grated Parmesan, dot with butter and roast in a preheated oven, 200°C (400°F), Gas Mark 6, for 15 minutes, until the cheese is bubbling and golden.

- Serve on a bed of rocket leaves, drizzled with balsamic syrup.

Cheese and Onion Bruschetta

Heat 1 tablespoon olive oil in a frying pan and sauté 1 large sliced onion for 2–3 minutes, until soft. Stir in ½ teaspoon sugar and 1 teaspoon balsamic vinegar and cook for a further 1–2 minutes. Toast 8 slices of ciabatta on both sides. Top each one with the caramelized onions and 100 g (3½ oz) crumbled Gorgonzola cheese. Cook under a preheated hot grill, until the cheese is golden and bubbling.

Onion Soup

Heat 2 tablespoons olive oil in a saucepan and cook 4 crushed garlic cloves, 4 sliced red onions, 2 sliced white onions, 4 sliced shallots and 3–4 sage leaves, covered, for 10–12 minutes, stirring occasionally. Sprinkle in 1 teaspoon sugar and 1 teaspoon balsamic vinegar and season well. Pour in 1.8 litres (3 pints) hot vegetable or chicken stock and simmer for 4–5 minutes. Serve with slices of cheese on toast.

Panzanella

Serves 4

300 g (10 oz) ripe tomatoes
125 g (4 oz) ciabatta bread
16 olives, pitted
3 teaspoons capers
½ red onion, finely sliced
300 g (10 oz) red and yellow
  cherry tomatoes, halved
6–8 basil leaves
1 tablespoon red wine vinegar
2 tablespoons olive oil

- Place the tomatoes in a sieve over a bowl. Using the back of a spoon, squash them well to release all the juice into the bowl.

- Roughly break up the bread and add it to the tomato juice. Leave to stand for 15 minutes, then transfer to a serving dish.

- Scatter the remaining ingredients over the bread, drizzling over the red wine vinegar and olive oil before serving.

Tomato Ciabatta Toasts

Toast 8 slices of ciabatta on both sides, then rub each slice with a garlic clove. Top the ciabatta slices with 300 g (10 oz) chopped tomatoes and 2 teaspoons capers. Sprinkle with chopped basil leaves and drizzle with olive oil.

Tomato Salad with Ciabatta Croûtons

Cut 1 ciabatta loaf into cubes. Heat 2 tablespoons olive oil in a frying pan and fry the cubes of bread until they are golden. Drain on kitchen paper. Toss the fried bread together with 300 g (10 oz) roughly chopped ripe

tomatoes, 16 pitted black olives, ½ sliced red onion, 300 g (10 oz) red and yellow cherry tomatoes, 6–8 torn basil leaves and 60 g (2¼ oz) baby spinach leaves. Drizzle with 2 tablespoons olive oil and 1 tablespoon red wine vinegar to serve.

Parmesan Crisps

Serves 4

150 g (5 oz) Parmesan cheese, grated

- Line 2 or 3 baking sheets with greaseproof paper. Place a 5 cm (2 inch) pastry cutter on the baking sheet and sprinkle 1 heaped teaspoon of the grated Parmesan inside the cutter to make a circular disc.

- Carefully remove the cutter and repeat with the remaining cheese, leaving 5 mm (¼ inch) between each disc.

- Bake in a preheated oven to 160°C (325°F), Gas Mark 3, for 8 minutes, until golden brown.

- Using a palette knife, transfer the crisps to a wire rack to cool.

- Store in an airtight container until required.

2 Parmesan Scones

Put 225 g (7½ oz) self-raising flour, 40 g (1¾ oz) butter and 20 g (¾ oz) grated Parmesan cheese in a food processor and process until it resembles fine breadcrumbs. Add 150 ml (¼ pint) milk and process until the dough comes together. Turn out on to a lightly floured work surface and gently roll or press out to a thickness of 2 cm (¾ inch). Cut out 8 scones using a 6 cm (2½ inch) biscuit cutter. Place them on a baking sheet, sprinkle with 10 g (⅓ oz) grated Parmesan and bake in a preheated oven, 220°C (425°F), Gas Mark 7, for 12–15 minutes, until golden.

3 Parmesan and Thyme Shortbread

Cream 75 g (3 oz) butter in a mixing bowl and then add 85 g (3¼ oz) plain flour, 85 g (3¼ oz) grated Parmesan, 2 teaspoons olive oil and 1½ teaspoons chopped thyme leaves. Using your hands, bring the mixture together into a dough. Roll the dough out on a lightly floured work surface to a thickness of 5 mm (¼ inch) and cut out about 18–20 rounds using a 4–5 cm (1¾–2 inch) biscuit cutter. Place the rounds on a baking sheet and chill for 15 minutes. Bake in a preheated oven, 180°C (350°F), Gas Mark 4, for 7–8 minutes, until lightly golden.

Broad Bean and Mint Soup

Serves 4

550 g (1 lb 3 oz) frozen broad beans, defrosted
2 tablespoons olive oil
2 shallots, peeled and diced
1 large carrot, peeled and diced
1 celery stick, diced
900 ml (1½ pints) vegetable stock
½ tablespoon chopped mint leaves
salt and pepper
4 tablespoons double cream, to serve

- Blanch the broad beans in boiling water for 3–4 minutes, then drain and refresh under cold water. Peel off the tough outer skins.

- Meanwhile, heat the olive oil in a saucepan and sauté the shallots, carrot and celery for 5–6 minutes. Stir in the skinned broad beans.

- Pour in the stock, bring to the boil and then simmer for 8–10 minutes.

- Stir in the mint and then, using a hand blender, or in a food processor or blender, blend the soup until smooth.

- Season to taste and serve with a swirl of cream.

---

1 Broad Bean Dip

Blanch 450 g (14½ oz) broad beans in boiling water for 3–4 minutes, then drain and refresh under cold water. Peel off the outer skins then place in a food processor or blender with 1 chopped red onion and a handful of mint leaves. Blend together. Stir in 350 g (11½ oz) crème fraîche, the juice of ½ lemon and some salt and pepper. Serve with toasted ciabatta slices.

3 Broad Bean, Pea and Mint Salad

Blanch 300 g (10 oz) broad beans and 200 g (7 oz) peas in a saucepan of boiling water for 3–4 minutes, then drain and refresh under cold water. Peel off the tough outer skins from the broad beans. Heat 2 tablespoons extra-virgin olive oil in a frying pan and fry 2 handfuls of cubed bread, 2 crushed garlic cloves and 2 teaspoons chopped basil leaves, until the croûtons are golden. Drain on kitchen paper. Heat a griddle pan until hot and cook 250 g (8 oz) sliced halloumi until it has marks on both sides. Whisk together 3 tablespoons extra-virgin olive oil, 1 tablespoon balsamic vinegar, 1 teaspoon wholegrain mustard and ½ teaspoon honey in a bowl. Toss the broad beans and peas with 2 tablespoons shredded mint leaves, 50 g (2 oz) rocket leaves and the croûtons. Top with the griddled halloumi and drizzle over the dressing to serve.

Chickpea and Chestnut Soup

Serves 4

1 tablespoon olive oil

2 celery sticks, chopped

2 garlic cloves, chopped

1 red chilli, deseeded and chopped

1 teaspoon chopped rosemary

400 g (13 oz) can chopped
tomatoes

400 g (13 oz) vacuum-packed
chestnuts

400 g (13 oz) can chickpeas,
rinsed and drained

400 ml (14 fl oz) vegetable stock

salt and pepper

To serve

2 tablespoons olive oil

2 tablespoons grated Parmesan
cheese

- Heat the olive oil in a saucepan and sauté the celery, garlic, chilli and rosemary for 2–3 minutes.

- Stir in the tomatoes, chestnuts and chickpeas with the stock and simmer for 8–10 minutes.

- Remove one-third of the soup and blend, using a hand blender, or in a food processor or blender, to give a thick consistency. Return to the pan, season and serve with a swirl of olive oil and sprinkled with grated Parmesan.

Chickpea, Chestnut and Feta Salad

Drain and rinse a 400 g (13 oz) can chickpeas, and toss together with ½ diced red chilli, 2 shredded baby gem lettuce, 100 g (3½ oz) quartered cherry tomatoes, 50 g (2 oz) chopped vacuum-packed chestnuts, 1 cored, deseeded and diced red pepper and 200 g (7 oz) crumbled feta cheese. Toss with 2–3 tablespoons Italian salad dressing and serve with crusty bread.

Pork Loin Chops with Chestnut

Sauce Heat 2 tablespoons olive oil in a frying pan and fry 100 g (3½ oz) diced pancetta for 4–5 minutes, then add 50 ml (2 fl oz) red wine and 200 g (7 oz) chopped vacuum-packed chestnuts. Pour in 150 ml (¼ pint) chicken stock and cook for 10–12 minutes, until the chestnuts are soft and breaking down. Blend the sauce in a food processor or blender and season to taste. Meanwhile, cook 125 g (4 oz) chopped potatoes and 150 g (5 oz) sweet potatoes in a saucepan of boiling water until tender. Add a 400 g (13 oz) can chickpeas, drained and rinsed, for the last 2 minutes of cooking, to heat through. Drain and roughly crush with a fork. Cook 4 x 150 g (5 oz) pork chops under a preheated hot grill for 3–4 minutes on each side and serve on top of the crushed potatoes with the chestnut sauce spooned over and sprinkled with torn sage leaves.

Aubergine Parmigiana

Serves 4

3 tablespoons olive oil
2 aubergines, sliced
1 onion, diced
2 garlic cloves, crushed
400 g (13 oz) can chopped
tomatoes
1 teaspoon chopped oregano
200 g (7 oz) mozzarella cheese,
grated
2 beef tomatoes, thinly sliced
6 tablespoons grated Parmesan
cheese

- Heat 2 tablespoon of the olive oil in a frying pan and cook the aubergine slices in batches, until golden.

- Heat the remaining oil in the pan and sauté the onion and garlic for 3–4 minutes. Stir in the tomatoes and oregano.

- Layer the aubergine slices in an ovenproof dish with the mozzarella and beef tomatoes.

- Pour over the tomato sauce and sprinkle with the grated Parmesan. Bake in a preheated oven, 200°C (400°F), Gas Mark 6, for 15–18 minutes. Serve warm.

1 Courgette and Tomato Gratin

Heat 2 tablespoons olive oil in a pan and sauté 3 sliced courgettes until golden. Layer with 4 sliced tomatoes, 6–8 roughly torn basil leaves and 200 g (7 oz) grated mozzarella in an ovenproof dish. Sprinkle with 2 tablespoons breadcrumbs and 4 tablespoons grated Parmesan. Bake in a preheated oven, 220°C (425°F), Gas Mark 7, for 5 minutes.

2 Ricotta-Stuffed Aubergine Rolls

Heat a griddle pan. When hot, griddle slices of aubergine that have been cut lengthways from 2 aubergines, for 2–3 minutes on each side, until golden. Mix together 150 g (5 oz) ricotta cheese, 150 g (5 oz) chopped mozzarella cheese, 2 teaspoons chopped basil leaves and 2 sliced spring onions. Place 1 teaspoon of the ricotta mixture on to the end of each slice of aubergine, then roll up each slice and place seam side down in an ovenproof dish. Pour over 300 g (10 oz) ready-made tomato sauce and bake in a preheated oven, 190°C (375°F), Gas Mark 5, for 12–15 minutes until the cheese starts to melt. Serve with a rocket salad.

Courgette Fritters with Poached Eggs

Serves 4

4 courgettes, grated
4 tablespoons self-raising flour
40 g (1¾ oz) Parmesan cheese, grated
2 tablespoons olive oil
4 eggs
pepper

- Place the grated courgette, flour and grated Parmesan in a bowl and mix together well.

- Squeeze into walnut-sized balls and then gently flatten.

- Heat the oil in a deep frying pan and, working in batches if necessary, fry the fritters for 2–3 minutes on each side, until golden.

- Meanwhile, bring a large saucepan of water to a gentle simmer and stir with a large spoon to create a swirl. Carefully break 2 eggs into the water and cook for 3 minutes. Remove with a slotted spoon and keep warm. Repeat with the remaining eggs.

- Serve the fritters topped with the poached eggs and sprinkled with pepper.

Griddled Courgettes with Mint and Lemon

Use a vegetable peeler to slice 4 courgettes very thinly, brush each slice with olive oil and sprinkle with 2 crushed garlic cloves. Heat a griddle pan until very hot and cook the slices for 2–3 minutes on each side, until charred (this can also be done on a hot barbecue grill). Place on a serving platter and scatter over the grated rind and juice of 1 lemon and 1 finely chopped green chilli. Toss gently. To serve, drizzle over 1 tablespoon olive oil and sprinkle with 2 tablespoons chopped mint leaves and 20 g (¾ oz) Parmesan shavings.

Courgette and Parmesan Soup

Heat 3 tablespoons olive oil in a saucepan and sauté 1 kg (2 lb) chopped courgettes with 2 chopped garlic cloves and a small handful of chopped basil leaves. Pour in 750 ml (1¼ pints) vegetable stock and bring to the boil. Simmer for 8–10 minutes and then remove from the heat. Stir in 4 tablespoons single cream. Using a hand blender, or in a food processor or blender, blend the soup until smooth. Stir in 50 g (2 oz) grated Parmesan cheese, season with pepper and reheat. Serve with crusty bread.

30 Stuffed Mushrooms

Serves 4

2 tablespoons olive oil

2 shallots, finely diced

1 garlic clove, crushed

175 g (6 oz) spinach leaves

175 g (6 oz) shop-bought
ready-cooked basmati rice

25 g (1 oz) Gorgonzola cheese,
chopped

4 large portabello mushrooms,
stalks trimmed

2 tablespoons grated Parmesan
cheese

crisp green salad, to serve

- Heat 1 tablespoon of the olive oil in a frying pan and sauté the shallot and garlic for 2–3 minutes.

- Stir in the spinach and cook until it has wilted. Take off the heat and stir in the rice and Gorgonzola and mix well.

- Place the mushrooms in a roasting tin and divide the spinach mixture between them. Sprinkle with the grated Parmesan.

- Drizzle with the remaining olive oil and bake in a preheated oven, 200°C (400°F), Gas Mark 6, for 18–20 minutes, until cooked.

- Serve with a crisp green salad.

---

10 Creamy Mushroom Toasts

Toast 8 slices of ciabatta on both sides, then rub each slice with a garlic clove. Heat 2 tablespoons olive oil in a frying pan and sauté 3 sliced spring onions and 300 g (10 oz) chestnut mushrooms for 3–4 minutes, until softened and just starting to brown. Stir in 1 tablespoon chopped parsley and 1 tablespoon crème fraîche, then spoon over the ciabatta slices and serve.

20 Fennel and Tomato Stuffed Mushrooms

Heat 2 frying pans, each with 1 tablespoon olive oil. In one pan, place 4 portabello mushrooms that have had the stalks removed. Cook over a low heat for 12–15 minutes. Meanwhile, cook the chopped mushroom stalks, 1 diced fennel bulb, 3 diced tomatoes and 3 sliced garlic cloves in the other pan for 5–6 minutes. Stir in 2 tablespoons breadcrumbs, 75 g (3 oz) crumbled Gorgonzola cheese and a small handful of shredded basil leaves. Spoon the mixture into the mushrooms and place on a baking sheet. Sprinkle with 2 tablespoons grated Parmesan cheese and cook under a preheated hot grill until golden.

QuickCook

Pizza, Pasta and More

Recipes listed by cooking time

3⏲

2⏲

Quick Artichoke and Salami Pizzas

Serves 4

4 flour tortillas
400 g (13 oz) passata
250 g (8 oz) salami, sliced
400 g (13 oz) can artichoke
  hearts, drained and sliced
6 sliced spring onions, sliced
1 teaspoon dried oregano
225 g (7½ oz) mozzarella, grated

- Place the tortillas on 2 baking sheets and warm in a preheated oven, 220°C (425°F), Gas Mark 7, for 2 minutes.

- Remove from the oven and spread each tortilla with passata and then top each one with some salami, sliced artichoke hearts, spring onions, oregano and mozzarella.

- Bake the pizzas for a further 3–5 minutes, until the tortilla edges are lightly browned and the mozzarella has melted.

 Orecchiette with Artichoke and Salami Cook 400 g (13 oz) orecchiette in a saucepan of boiling water according to the packet instructions, until 'al dente'. Meanwhile, heat 1 tablespoon olive oil in a saucepan and add 100 g (3½ oz) sliced salami, cut into strips, for 1–2 minutes. Stir in a 400 g (13 oz) can chopped tomatoes, 125 ml (4 fl oz) vegetable stock and a 400 g (13 oz) can artichoke hearts, drained and halved. Simmer for 5–6 minutes. Drain the pasta and add it to the salami sauce. Serve sprinkled with grated Parmesan cheese.

Artichoke and Red Pepper Pizza Place 1 kg (2 lb) strong bread flour, 2 x 7 g (¼ oz) sachets dried yeast and a pinch of salt in a large bowl and mix together. Stir in 2 tablespoons olive oil and about 600 ml (1 pint) warm water and mix together using your hands, until you have a soft, but not sticky dough. Turn the dough out on to a floured work surface and knead for 5–8 minutes. Divide into 4 pieces and roll out to 30 cm (12 inch) circles, then place on baking sheets. Spread each one with 100 g (3½ oz) passata, then divide a 400 g (13 oz) can artichoke hearts and 125 g (4 oz) roasted red peppers from a jar, both drained and sliced, between the pizzas. Sprinkle over 200 g (7 oz) grated mozzarella cheese and cook in a preheated oven, 220°C (425°F), Gas Mark 7, for 6–7 minutes.

30 Potato Gnocchi

Serves 4

800 g (1 lb 12 oz) floury potatoes, peeled and diced

1 egg yolk, beaten

150 g (5 oz) plain flour

15 g (½ oz) basil leaves, finely shredded

50 g (2 oz) Parmesan cheese, grated

4 tablespoons extra-virgin olive oil

salt and pepper

- Cook the potatoes in a saucepan of boiling water for 12–15 minutes, until soft. Drain and mash, or use a potato ricer to get a really smooth texture. Place another saucepan of water on the heat to boil.

- Transfer the mashed potato to a bowl and mix in the egg yolk, flour and basil. Mix well to combine.

- Take a teaspoon of the mixture into your hand and roll into a walnut-sized ball. Press with the prongs of a fork to make a gnocchi shape. Repeat with the remaining mixture.

- Drop the gnocchi into the saucepan of boiling water to cook – this should take only 1–2 minutes and the gnocchi will float when cooked.

- Toss the hot gnocchi in the grated Parmesan and olive oil and serve immediately.

---

10 Potato Gnocchi in a Quick Tomato

Sauce Heat 1 tablespoon olive oil in a frying pan and sauté 2 diced shallots and 2 crushed garlic cloves for 1–2 minutes. Add a 400 g (13 oz) can chopped tomatoes, a pinch of dried chilli flakes, 2 teaspoons thyme leaves and 2 tablespoons white wine. Simmer for 5–6 minutes. Meanwhile, cook 800 g (1 lb 12 oz) ready-made gnocchi for 2 minutes in a saucepan of boiling water. Drain and toss the cooked gnocchi in the tomato sauce and serve sprinkled with Parmesan cheese shavings.

20 Potatoes with Pancetta and

Capers Cook 1 kg (2 lb) chopped potatoes in a saucepan of boiling water until tender. Meanwhile, heat 2 tablespoons olive oil and 25 g (1 oz) butter in a frying pan and sauté 1 chopped onion and 125 g (4 oz) diced pancetta for 5–6 minutes. Stir in 1 tablespoon chopped rosemary and 2 tablespoons capers. Drain the potatoes, add to the caper mixture and lightly crush in the pan. Bring a large saucepan of water to a gentle simmer and stir with a large spoon to create a swirl. Carefully break 2 eggs into the water and cook for 3 minutes. Remove with a slotted spoon and keep warm. Repeat with another 2 eggs. Stir 1 tablespoon chopped basil into the potatoes and divide between 4 warmed bowls. Top each one with a poached egg and sprinkle with 2 tablespoons grated Parmesan cheese.

Bacon Carbonara

Serves 4

400 g (13 oz) spaghetti
25 g (1 oz) butter
3 garlic cloves, finely diced
2 shallots, finely diced
8 streaky bacon rashers, chopped
4 eggs
200 ml (7 fl oz) single cream
40 g (1¾ oz) Parmesan cheese,
    grated

- Cook the spaghetti in a saucepan of boiling water according to the packet instructions, until 'al dente'.

- Meanwhile, heat the butter in a large frying pan and fry the garlic, shallots and bacon for 5–7 minutes, until golden.

- Beat together the eggs, cream and half the grated Parmesan.

- Using tongs, transfer the cooked spaghetti to the frying pan – don't worry if some of the cooking liquid comes with it.

- Pour in the egg mixture and toss the spaghetti until well coated, adding more cooking liquid if necessary.

- Serve sprinkled with the remaining Parmesan.

Quick Bacon and Egg Spaghetti

Cook 400 g (13 oz) quick-cook spaghetti in a saucepan of boiling water for 7–8 minutes, or according to the packet instructions, until 'al dente'. Meanwhile, heat 1 tablespoon olive oil in a frying pan and cook 8 chopped streaky bacon rashers until crisp. Beat together 4 eggs, 200 ml (7 fl oz) single cream and 40 g (1¾ oz) grated Parmesan cheese in a bowl or jug. Drain the pasta, then return to the pan and add the egg mixture and bacon. Toss together until the spaghetti is well coated. Season with salt and pepper and serve sprinkled with extra grated Parmesan.

Bacon and Pine Nut Pasta with Poached Eggs

Bring a large saucepan of water to a gentle simmer and stir with a large spoon to create a swirl. Carefully break 2 eggs into the water and cook for 3 minutes. Remove with a slotted spoon and repeat with another 2 eggs. Keep them warm. Cook 400 g (13 oz) tagliatelle in a saucepan of boiling water according to the packet instructions, until 'al dente'. Meanwhile, heat 1 tablespoon olive oil in a frying pan and fry 175 g (6 oz) bacon rashers, cut into strips, for 2 minutes. Add 200 g (7 oz) frozen peas, 2 tablespoons vegetable stock, 4 tablespoons crème fraîche and 4 sliced spring onions. Stir well and bring to a gentle simmer. Continue to cook for 3–4 minutes. Drain the pasta, transfer to the frying pan and gently toss in the creamy bacon sauce. Divide the pasta between 4 shallow bowls and top each one with a poached egg. Serve sprinkled with 2 tablespoons grated Parmesan and pepper.

ITA-PIZZ-CYI

Mushroom Risotto

Serves 4

10 g (⅓ oz) dried porcini
200 ml (7 fl oz) boiling water
1 tablespoon olive oil
2 shallots, diced
350 g (11½ oz) Arborio rice
150 ml (¼ pint) white wine
600 ml (1 pint) hot stock
175 g (6 oz) chestnut mushrooms
1 teaspoon chopped thyme leaves
salt and pepper
2 tablespoons grated Parmesan
   cheese, to serve

- Place the dried porcini in a bowl and cover with the measurement water. Leave to stand for 15 minutes.

- Meanwhile, heat the olive oil in a saucepan and sauté the shallots for 2–3 minutes, unitl softened but not coloured.

- Stir in the rice and continue to stir, until the edges of the grains look translucent.

- Pour in the wine, and cook for 1–2 minutes over a high heat and stir until it is absorbed.

- Add a ladle of the hot stock, reduce the heat to medium, and stir continuously until it has been absorbed. Repeat with the remaining hot stock, a ladle at a time.

- Drain the porcini, reserving the liquid. Roughly chop the porcini and add to the rice with the fresh mushrooms and a ladle of the porcini liquid.

- Continue to stir and add liquid, until the rice is 'al dente'.

- Stir in the thyme and season to taste.

- Serve sprinkled with grated Parmesan.

---

1 **Quick Mushroom Rice**

Heat 2 tablespoons olive oil in a frying pan and fry 350 g (11½ oz) chestnut mushrooms and 4 sliced spring onions for 5–6 minutes. Stir in a 400 g (13 oz) pack ready-cooked rice and 1 tablespoon chopped parsley. Season and serve sprinkled with 2 tablespoons grated Parmesan.

2 **Rice and Mushroom Soup**

Heat 2 tablespoons olive oil in a saucepan and sauté 2 chopped leeks and 2 sliced garlic cloves for 4–5 minutes, until softened. Add 300 g (10 oz) chopped chestnut mushrooms, 50 g (2 oz) long grain rice and 2 teaspoons thyme leaves and cook for a further 2–3 minutes.

Pour in 1.2 litres (2 pints) hot vegetable stock and simmer for 5 minutes. Using a hand blender, or in a food processor or blender, blend the soup until smooth. Season to taste and serve with crusty bread.

Fiorentina Pizzas

Serves 4

2 large ready-made pizza bases
500 g (1 lb) passata
2 tablespoons olive oil
2 garlic cloves, sliced
1 red onion, sliced
500 g (1 lb) spinach leaves
4 eggs
2 tablespoons pine nuts
200 g (7 oz) mozzarella cheese, grated
pepper

- Place the pizza bases on 2 baking sheets and spread each one with passata.

- Heat the olive oil in a large frying pan and sauté the garlic and onion for 2–3 minutes, then add the spinach and stir until it has completely wilted.

- Spread the wilted spinach over the pizza bases and make 2 small hollows in each pizza topping. Break the eggs into the hollows.

- Sprinkle each pizza with pine nuts, mozzarella and pepper.

- Bake in a preheated oven, 200°C (400°F), Gas Mark 6, for 12–15 minutes, until the eggs are cooked. Cut into slices and serve immediately.

10 Healthy Pitta Pizzas

Lightly poach 4 eggs. Toast 4 wholemeal pitta breads under a preheated hot grill for 1–2 minutes on each side, then spread with 1 tablespoon tomato ketchup. Heat 1 tablespoon olive oil in a frying pan, add 400 g (13 oz) spinach leaves and fry until wilted. Spread the spinach over the pitta breads. Top each one with a poached egg, then sprinkle with 1 tablespoon each of pine nuts and grated mozzarella. Cook under the hot grill for 3–4 minutes until the cheese melts.

30 Homemade Fiorentina Pizzas

Mix together 1 kg (2 lb) strong bread flour, 2 x 7 g (¼ oz) sachets dried yeast and a pinch of salt. Stir in 2 tablespoons olive oil and 1–2 tablespoons warm water. Mix together with your hand, gradually adding about 600 ml (1 pint) warm water, until you have a soft, but not sticky dough. Turn the dough out on to a lightly floured work surface and knead for 5–8 minutes, until the dough is smooth and elastic. Divide into 4 pieces and roll into 30 cm (12 inch) circles, then place on 2 baking sheets. Heat 2 tablespoons olive oil in a frying pan, add 500 g (1 lb) spinach leaves and fry until wilted. Spread 500 g (1 lb) passata over the pizza bases, followed by the spinach. Crack an egg into the centre of each pizza, sprinkle over 200 g (7 oz) grated mozzarella cheese and cook in a preheated oven, 220°C (425°F), Gas Mark 7, for 6–7 minutes, until the eggs are cooked.

Pappardelle with Creamy Asparagus and Herbs

Serves 4

450 g (14½ oz) asparagus, trimmed and cut into 2.5 cm (1 inch) lengths
400 g (13 oz) pappardelle
1 tablespoon olive oil
1 onion, diced
2 garlic cloves, crushed
300 ml (10 fl oz) single cream
¼ teaspoon grated nutmeg
2 tablespoons each of chopped basil, parsley and chives
2 tablespoons grated Parmesan cheese, to serve

- Blanch the asparagus in a saucepan of boiling water for 3–4 minutes. Drain and keep warm.

- Cook the pappardelle in a saucepan of boiling water according to the packet instructions, until 'al dente'.

- Meanwhile, heat the olive oil in a frying pan and sauté the onion and garlic for 4–5 minutes.

- Stir in the cream and simmer for 6–8 minutes, until the cream has reduced and thickened a little. Stir in the grated nutmeg.

- Drain the pasta and add to the cream sauce with the asparagus and herbs. Toss together gently.

- Serve sprinkled with grated Parmesan.

---

1 Asparagus Pasta Salad

Cook 200 g (7 oz) fresh penne in a saucepan of boiling water according to the packet instructions, until 'al dente', then drain and refresh under cold water. Meanwhile, steam 350 g (11½ oz) halved asparagus tips until tender, then drain and refresh under cold water. Place the pasta and asparagus in a salad bowl and toss together with 100 g (3½ oz) chopped cherry tomatoes, 125 g (4 oz) roasted red peppers from a jar, drained and sliced, 100 g (3½ oz) chopped mozzarella cheese, 1 tablespoon chopped basil leaves and some Italian salad dressing.

2 Asparagus Pesto Pasta

Cook 400 g (13 oz) tagliatelle in a saucepan of boiling water according to the packet instructions, until 'al dente'. Meanwhile, cook 500 g (1 lb) trimmed asparagus in a saucepan of boiling water for 2–3 minutes, then drain. Place the asparagus, 125 g (4 oz) spinach leaves, 30 g (1¼ oz) grated Parmesan cheese, 2 crushed garlic cloves and 2 tablespoons toasted pine nuts in a food processor and blitz for 30 seconds, then pour in 3–4 tablespoons extra virgin olive oil with the motor still running until a thick paste forms. Add the juice of ½ lemon and a little water to loosen and season to taste. Drain the pasta, return to the pan and add the asparagus pesto. Toss together. Serve sprinkled with extra toasted pine nuts.

Crab Linguine

Serves 4

450 g (14½ oz) linguine
125 ml (4 fl oz) olive oil
2 garlic cloves, crushed
1 red chilli, deseeded and
   finely diced
grated rind and juice of 1 lemon
250 g (8 oz) white crab meat
2 tablespoons chopped parsley

- Cook the linguine in a large saucepan of boiling water according to the packet instructions, until 'al dente'.

- Meanwhile, in another large saucepan, heat the olive oil and cook the garlic, chilli and lemon rind over a low heat for 3–4 minutes.

- Drain the pasta and add it to the olive oil pan along with the lemon juice, crab meat and the chopped parsley. Toss together gently to warm the crab through, and then serve.

Crab Pasta Salad

Cook 300 g (10 oz) fresh fusilli in a saucepan of boiling water according to the packet instructions, until 'al dente', then drain and refresh under cold water. Meanwhile, steam 125 g (4 oz) broccoli florets until just tender, then drain and refresh under cold water. Place the pasta and broccoli in a salad bowl and toss together with 1 cored, deseeded and sliced red pepper, 4 sliced spring onions, 2 chopped plum tomatoes and 250 g (8 oz) white crab meat. Toss together with some Italian salad dressing and serve with crusty bread.

Crab Tart

Whisk together 4 eggs and 125 ml (4 fl oz) single cream in a bowl. Stir in 225 g (7½ oz) white crab meat, ½ diced red chilli, 4 chopped spring onions, 1 cored, deseeded and finely sliced red pepper, 1 tablespoon chopped parsley and 25 g (1 oz) grated Parmesan. Pour the mixture into a 23 cm (9 inch) shop-bought shortcrust pastry case and sprinkle over another 25 g (1 oz) grated Parmesan. Bake in a preheated oven, 200°C (400°F), Gas Mark 6, for 22–25 minutes.

Tricolori Pitta Pizzas

Serves 4

4 pitta breads
1 tablespoon olive oil
350 g (11½ oz) spinach leaves
4 tablespoons tomato ketchup
2 yellow peppers, cored,
    deseeded and finely sliced
250 g (8 oz) roasted red peppers
    from a jar, drained and sliced
250 g (8 oz) mozzarella cheese,
    grated

- Cook the pitta bread under a preheated hot grill for 1–2 minutes. While they are still warm, run a knife down one side and split them open to give 2 flat pieces of bread.

- Meanwhile, heat the olive oil in a frying pan and add the spinach. Stir for 1–2 minutes, until it starts to wilt.

- Spread 1 tablespoon of the ketchup on each flatbread. Top with the spinach, sliced yellow and red peppers and finally the mozzarella.

- Cook under a preheated hot grill for 4–5 minutes, until the cheese is melted and golden.

2 Tricolori Pizzas

Using 2 medium ready-made pizza bases, spread each one with 2 tablespoons passata. Top each one with 1 sliced tomato, ½ each of red and yellow peppers, deseeded and sliced, ¼ thinly sliced red onion and 50 g (2 oz) of grated mozzarella cheese. Sprinkle with 6–8 shredded basil leaves and bake in a preheated oven, 200°C (400°F) Gas Mark 6, for 11–13 minutes. Cut into wedges and serve with a crisp green salad.

3 Tricolori Frittata

Heat 2 tablespoons olive oil in a flameproof frying pan and cook 1 sliced red onion, 1 red pepper and 1 yellow pepper, each cored, deseeded and sliced, and 2 crushed garlic cloves for 3–4 minutes, until tender, then add 200 g (7 oz) baby spinach leaves and stir until they are completely wilted. Beat together 7 eggs, 1 tablespoon milk and some salt and pepper, then pour into the pan. Stir the mixture around to ensure it all reaches the base of the pan. Cook over a low heat for 20 minutes, or until the bottom is set (use a palette knife to pull away at the edges to check), then cook under a preheated hot grill, until golden. Turn out on to a board and cut into wedges to serve.

ITA-PIZZ-VAE

Broccoli and Chilli Orecchiette

Serves 4

350 g (11½ oz) broccoli, cut into florets

300 g (10 oz) orecchiette

4 tablespoons olive oil

3 shallots, diced

4 garlic cloves, finely chopped

1 teaspoon dried chilli flakes

2 tablespoons chopped parsley

2 tablespoons Parmesan cheese shavings, to serve

- Steam the broccoli for 4–5 minutes, until just tender. Drain.

- Cook the orecchiette in a saucepan of boiling water for 11–13 minutes, until 'al dente'.

- Meanwhile, heat 2 tablespoons of the olive oil in a frying pan and sauté the shallots with the garlic and chilli flakes for 3–4 minutes.

- Add the broccoli to the frying pan and stir to coat with the spicy oil.

- Drain the pasta and add to the frying pan with the remaining oil and chopped parsley. Toss together well.

- Serve sprinkled with Parmesan shavings.

---

1 Broccoli and Tuna Pasta Bake

Cook 200 g (7 oz) fresh penne in a saucepan of boiling water according to the packet instructions, until 'al dente'. Meanwhile, steam 300 g (10 oz) broccoli florets for 4–5 minutes until just tender. Drain the penne and broccoli and mix together in an ovenproof dish with 4 chopped tomatoes and a drained 400 g (13 oz) can tuna. Pour over 350 ml (12 fl oz) warmed ready-made cheese sauce and sprinkle with 4 tablespoons fresh breadcrumbs and 2 tablespoons grated Parmesan cheese. Place under a preheated hot grill for 3–4 minutes until golden. Serve with a crisp green salad.

3 Broccoli and Bacon Pasta Salad

Halve, core and deseed 2 red peppers and cook, cut side down, under a preheated hot grill for 6–7 minutes, until the skin turns black. Place in a bowl, cover with clingfilm and leave until cool enough to handle. Meanwhile, cook 250 g (8 oz) orecchiette in a saucepan of boiling water according to the packet instructions, until 'al dente', then drain. Grill 8 streaky bacon rashers until crisp and then roughly chop. Cut 2 heads of broccoli into florets and steam for 2–3 minutes, until just tender. Peel away the blackened skin from the peppers, then cut into strips. Quarter and deseed 3 tomatoes, then cut into strips.

For the dressing, whisk together 5 tablespoons extra virgin olive oil, 2 tablespoons white wine vinegar, 2 teaspoons Dijon mustard, ½ crushed garlic clove and 1 diced red chilli in a small bowl, then season with salt and pepper. Toss together the pasta, vegetables, bacon and 50 g (2 oz) watercress in a large bowl, then pour over the dressing to serve.

Spaghetti Bolognese with Griddled Cherry Tomatoes

Serves 4

1 tablespoon olive oil
2 streaky bacon rashers, chopped
1 large onion, chopped
2 garlic cloves, crushed
500 g (1 lb) minced beef
150 ml (¼ pint) red wine
400 g (13 oz) can chopped
  tomatoes
½ teaspoon dried oregano
400 g (13 oz) spaghetti
4 small vines of cherry tomatoes
4 tablespoons grated Parmesan
  cheese, to serve

- Heat the olive oil in a frying pan and fry the bacon until golden. Add the onion and garlic and cook for 2–3 minutes, until the onion is softened.

- Increase the heat, add the minced beef and cook to brown.

- Pour in the wine and boil until it has reduced in volume by half and then add the tomatoes and oregano. Simmer for 20–22 minutes.

- Meanwhile, cook the spaghetti in a saucepan of boiling water according to the packet instructions, until 'al dente'.

- Heat a griddle pan and cook the vine cherry tomatoes for 3–4 minutes.

- Drain the pasta and divide between 4 bowls. Spoon over the Bolognese sauce, top with a vine of cherry tomatoes and serve sprinkled with grated Parmesan.

1 Spaghetti with Tomatoes

Cook 400 g (13 oz) spaghetti in a saucepan of boiling water according to the packet instructions, until 'al dente'. Meanwhile, heat 4 tablespoons olive oil in a frying pan and sauté 1 diced shallot, 1 crushed garlic clove and 5 chopped plum tomatoes. Drain the pasta and toss with the tomatoes. Stir in 3 tablespoons chopped basil leaves and serve sprinkled with grated Parmesan cheese.

2 Tomato and Bolognese Pizza

Heat 1 tablespoon olive oil in a saucepan, add 1 chopped onion and 500 g (1 lb) minced beef and cook for 4–5 minutes, until browned. Stir in 250 g (8 oz) ready-made tomato pasta sauce and simmer for 3–4 minutes. Spoon the meat over 4 ready-made pizza bases, top with 2 sliced tomatoes, sprinkle with 4 tablespoons grated Mozzarella and bake in a preheated oven, 220°C (425°F), Gas Mark 7, for 10–11 minutes, until the cheese is melted and golden.

Pea and Mint Risotto

Serves 4

1 tablespoon olive oil

2 shallots, finely diced

400 g (13 oz) Arborio rice

100 ml (3½ fl oz) white wine

about 900 ml (1½ pints) hot
  vegetable stock

100 g (3½ oz) fresh or frozen
  peas, defrosted

a small handful of mint leaves,
  chopped

40 g (1¾ oz) butter

40 g (1¾ oz) Parmesan cheese,
  grated

salt and pepper

- Heat the olive oil in a large saucepan and sauté the shallots for 2–3 minutes, until softened but not coloured.

- Stir in the rice and continue to stir, until the edges of the grains look translucent.

- Pour in the wine and cook for 1–2 minutes, until it is absorbed.

- Add a ladle of the hot vegetable stock and stir continuously, until it has all been absorbed.

- Repeat with the remaining hot stock, adding a ladle at a time, until the rice is 'al dente'.

- Stir in the peas, mint, butter and half the Parmesan, season with salt and pepper and cook for a further 2–3 minutes.

- Serve sprinkled with the remaining grated Parmesan.

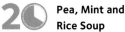

Pea and Mint Pasta Salad

Cook 200 g (7 oz) fresh penne in a saucepan of boiling water according to the packet instructions, until 'al dente', then drain and refresh under cold water. Meanwhile, cook 350 g (11½ oz) frozen peas in boiling water for 3–4 minutes, then drain and refresh under cold water. Toss the pasta and peas with 100 g (3½ oz) halved cherry tomatoes, 1 tablespoon chopped mint leaves, 125 g (4 oz) chopped mozzarella cheese and 2 tablespoons pitted black olives in a salad bowl. Add 125 g (4 oz) baby spinach leaves and 3–4 tablespoons Italian salad dressing and toss together gently.

Pea, Mint and Rice Soup

Heat 2 tablespoons olive oil in a large saucepan and sauté 2 peeled and diced shallots and 1 diced celery stick for 4–5 minutes, until softened. Pour in 600 ml (1 pint) vegetable stock, bring to a simmer and add 400 g (13 oz) fresh or frozen peas. Cook for 10 minutes, or until the peas are tender. Add 2 tablespoons roughly chopped mint leaves. Using a hand blender, or in a food processor or blender, blend the soup until smooth. Stir in 125 g (4 oz) shop-bought ready-cooked risotto of your choice, season to taste and heat through until piping hot. Serve topped with a swirl of double cream or natural yogurt and 2 teaspoons chopped mint leaves.

Penne Arrabbiata

Serves 4

4 tablespoons olive oil
2 red chillies, finely sliced
2 garlic cloves, chopped
600 g (1¼ lb) canned chopped tomatoes
6–8 basil leaves, shredded
400 g (13 oz) penne
salt and pepper
25 g (1 oz) Parmesan cheese, grated, to serve

- Heat the olive oil in a large frying pan, add the red chillies and garlic and cook for 2–3 minutes.

- Add the chopped tomatoes and basil and simmer for 12 minutes. Season to taste.

- Meanwhile, cook the penne in a saucepan of boiling water according to the packet instructions, until 'al dente'. Drain the pasta and add it to the tomato sauce. Stir until combined.

- Serve sprinkled with grated Parmesan.

Quick Spicy Tomato Pasta

Heat 2 tablespoons olive oil in a large frying pan and sauté 1 diced shallot and 1 finely diced red chilli, until softened, then add 3–4 chopped plum tomatoes and 1 tablespoon chopped basil leaves. Meanwhile, cook 300 g (10 oz) fresh conchiglie in a saucepan of boiling water according to the packet instructions, until 'al dente', then drain. Remove the tomato mixture from the heat and stir in the pasta and 1 tablespoon balsamic vinegar. Place 60 g (2¼ oz) watercress on a serving platter and spoon over the tomato pasta. Serve sprinkled with 2 tablespoons grated mozzarella cheese and 2 tablespoons toasted pine nuts.

Chilli Tomato Tart

Roll out 300 g (10 oz) shop-bought chilled puff pastry on a lightly floured work surface to 25 cm (10 inches) square. Place on a baking sheet and score a square about 2.5 cm (1 inch) in from the edge. Bake in a preheated oven, 200°C (400°F), Gas Mark 6, for 10 minutes, until golden. Slice 600 g (1¼ lb) plum tomatoes and lay them on the centre of the pastry. Sprinkle with ½ teaspoon dried chilli flakes, 1 tablespoon chopped black olives and 1 tablespoon grated Parmesan. Bake for a further 10–12 minutes and serve with steamed green beans and courgettes.

ITA-PIZZ-BUP

Fettucine with Dolcelatte and Spinach

Serves 4

400 g (13 oz) fettucine
1 tablespoon olive oil
1 onion, chopped
2 garlic cloves, crushed
300 ml (½ pint) single cream
125 g (4 oz) dolcelatte cheese
150 g (5 oz) baby spinach leaves
salt and pepper

- Cook the fettucine in a saucepan of boiling water according to the packet instructions, until 'al dente'.

- Meanwhile, heat the olive oil in a frying pan and sauté the onion and garlic for 4–5 minutes. Pour in the cream and simmer for 5–6 minutes, until the cream thickens a little.

- Stir in the dolcelatte and spinach and stir for 1 minute. Drain the pasta and add to the spinach. Season with salt and pepper then gently mix together and serve in warmed bowls.

Dolcelatte and Spinach Pizzas

Toast 4 wholemeal pitta breads under a preheated hot grill for 1–2 minutes on each side. Spread each one with 1 tablespoon tomato ketchup. Meanwhile, heat 1 tablespoon olive oil in a frying pan, add 400 g (13 oz) spinach leaves and cook until wilted. Divide between the pitta breads. Top each with 40 g (1¾ oz) crumbled dolcelatte cheese, then sprinkle over 1 tablespoon pine nuts. Cook under a preheated grill for 3–4 minutes, until the cheese is melted. Serve topped with a small handful of rocket leaves.

Dolcelatte and Spinach Soup

Heat 1 tablespoon olive oil in a saucepan and sauté 1 chopped onion and 2 chopped garlic cloves for 3–4 minutes. Stir in 1 chopped potato and cook for a further 1–2 minutes. Pour in 450 ml (¾ pint) vegetable stock and bring to the boil. Simmer for 10 minutes and then stir in 600 ml (1 pint) milk and bring to a simmer again. Add 225 g (7½ oz) baby spinach leaves and the grated rind of 1 lemon and cook for 5–6 minutes, then stir in another 225 g (7½ oz) baby spinach leaves and 50 g (2 oz) dolcelatte. Using a hand blender, or in a food processor or blender, blend the soup until smooth. Season and serve the soup with toasted pumpkin seeds and a few more crumbs of dolcelatte.

3 Saffron Risotto

Serves 4

2 tablespoons olive oil
1 onion, finely diced
300 g (10 oz) Arborio rice
200 ml (7 fl oz) white wine
750 ml (1¼ pints) hot chicken stock
2 pinches of saffron strands
25 g (1 oz) butter
40 g (1½ oz) Parmesan cheese, grated

- Heat the olive oil in a saucepan and sauté the onion for 3–5 minutes until softened.

- Stir in the rice and continue to stir, until the edges of the grains look translucent. Pour in the wine and cook for 1–2 minutes, until it is absorbed.

- Add a ladle of the hot chicken stock and the saffron and stir continuously, until it has all been absorbed. Repeat with the remaining hot stock, adding a ladle at a time, until the rice is 'al dente'.

- Remove from the heat and stir in the butter and half the grated Parmesan.

- Serve sprinkled with the remaining Parmesan.

1 Warm Saffron Rice Salad

Heat 2 tablespoons olive oil in a frying pan and cook 1 large chopped onion and 3 crushed garlic cloves for 4–5 minutes, until golden. Stir in 300 g (10 oz) pack ready-cooked long grain rice and heat through until piping hot. Meanwhile, crumble 1 large pinch of saffron threads into a small saucepan, add 3 tablespoons hot vegetable stock and simmer for 1 minute, until infused, then stir into the rice with 2 tablespoons sultanas, 3 tablespoons toasted flaked almonds, 2 tablespoons pitted green olives, 1 tablespoon chopped mint leaves and 2 tablespoons chopped parsley.

2 Saffron Scrambled Egg

Heat 200 ml (7 fl oz) milk in a saucepan with a large pinch of saffron threads. Cover and leave to stand for 4 minutes. Whisk together 8 large eggs with some salt and pepper in a bowl and then add the saffron milk. Heat 25 g (1 oz) butter in a nonstick frying pan and pour in the egg mixture. Let it sit without stirring for 20 seconds, then stir with a wooden spoon. Repeat this process, stirring and folding, until the egg is nearly cooked. Leave to stand for 2 minutes. Meanwhile, toast 8 slices of ciabatta on both sides. Spoon the egg over the toast to serve.

Penne with Walnut Sauce

Serves 4

2 tablespoons olive oil
3 shallots, diced
150 g (5 oz) walnut pieces
350 g (11½ oz) penne
2 tablespoons mascarpone
   cheese
3 tablespoons natural yogurt
2 tablespoons chopped parsley
pepper
30 g (1¼ oz) Parmesan cheese,
   grated, to serve

- Heat the olive oil in a frying pan and sauté the shallots for 2–3 minutes.

- Place half the walnuts in a food processor or blender and process until fine.

- Add the remaining walnuts to the frying pan and cook for 5–6 minutes.

- Meahwhile, cook the penne in a saucepan of boiling water according to the packet instructions, until 'al dente'.

- Stir the ground walnuts, mascarpone and yogurt into the frying pan and stir until smooth. Stir in the chopped parsley and simmer gently for a few minutes.

- Drain the pasta, reserving 2 tablespoons of the cooking liquid. Add the pasta and liquid to the walnut sauce and toss together gently. Add pepper to taste.

- Serve sprinkled with grated Parmesan.

---

10 Walnut Penne Pesto

Cook 400 g (13 oz) penne according to the packet instructions, until 'al dente'. Meanwhile, Put 175 g (6 oz) walnut pieces and 1 crushed garlic clove in a food processor or blender and process until finely chopped. Add a handful of basil leaves, 100 g (3½ oz) grated Parmesan, 2 teaspoons lemon juice and 4 tablespoons olive oil and process again until nearly smooth. Add a little more olive oil if needed to loosen the mixture. Drain the pasta and serve with the pesto.

30 Baked Tomato and Walnut Penne

Cook 400 g (13 oz) penne in a saucepan of boiling water according to the packet instructions, until 'al dente'. Meanwhile, heat 2 tablespoons olive oil in a saucepan and sauté 1 chopped onion, 2 chopped garlic cloves and 1 teaspoon dried chilli flakes for 2–3 minutes. Add 1.75 kg (3½ lb) skinned, deseeded and chopped ripe tomatoes and 100 ml (3½ fl oz) red wine and simmer for 6–8 minutes. Using a hand blender, or in a food processor or blender, blend the tomato mixture to a chunky sauce and return to the pan. Stir in 3 teaspoons shredded basil leaves, 3 tablespoons chopped walnuts and some salt and pepper. Drain the pasta and toss in the tomato sauce. Pour half the pasta into an ovenproof dish and sprinkle with 2 tablespoons grated Parmesan cheese and lay 125 g (4 oz) sliced mozzarella cheese on top. Pour in the remaining pasta and repeat with the cheeses. Bake in a preheated oven, 200°C (400°F), Gas Mark 6, for 12–15 minutes. Serve with a rocket salad.

30 Tomato Risotto

Serves 4

1 tablespoon olive oil

1 onion, diced

2 garlic cloves, crushed

100 g (3½ oz) plum tomatoes

200 ml (7 fl oz) ready-made
tomato sauce

300 ml (½ pint) hot vegetable
stock

200 g (7 oz) Arborio rice

50 g (2 oz) sun-dried tomatoes,
cut into strips

2 tablespoons shredded
basil leaves

salt and pepper

40 g (1¾ oz) grated Parmesan
cheese, to serve

- Heat the olive oil in a saucepan and sauté the onion and garlic for 5–6 minutes.

- Meanwhile, place the tomatoes in a large bowl and pour over boiling water. Leave to stand for 30 seconds, then drain and refresh under cold water. Peel off the skins, then deseed and chop the tomatoes.

- Place the tomato sauce and stock in a small saucepan and bring to a simmer.

- Stir the rice into the onions and continue to stir, for 1–2 minutes until the edges of the grains look translucent.

- Add a ladle of the tomato sauce and stock and stir continuously, until it has all been absorbed.

- Repeat with the remaining hot stock, adding a ladle at a time, until the rice is 'al dente'.

- Stir in the chopped tomatoes, sliced sun-dried tomatoes and basil and season to taste.

- Serve sprinkled with grated Parmesan.

---

1 **Quick Tomato and Rice Salad**

Skin and chop 4 plum tomatoes, as above, and mix with 4 sliced spring onions, 400 g (13 oz) shop-bought ready-cooked rice, 200 g (7 oz) diced mozzarella cheese and 2 tablespoons chopped basil leaves. Season and sprinkle with 2 tablespoons olive oil to serve.

2 **Tomato and Rice Soup**

Heat 3 tablespoons olive oil in a large saucepan and sauté 1 chopped onion, 1 diced carrot, 1 celery stick and 3 chopped garlic cloves for 3–4 minutes. Stir in ½ teaspoon fennel seeds, the grated rind of 1 orange, 2 tablespoons tomato purée, a 400 g (13 oz) can chopped tomatoes, 300 ml (½ pint) vegetable stock and 100 g (3½ oz) long grain rice. Season and simmer for 13–14 minutes, until the rice is cooked. Stir in 1 tablespoon shredded basil leaves to serve.

Sweetcorn and Spinach Polenta

Serves 4

1 tablespoon olive oil, plus extra
  to serve
4 spring onions, sliced
200 g (7 oz) frozen sweetcorn
800 ml (1¼ pints) hot vegetable
  stock
200 g (7 oz) instant polenta
a large handful of spinach leaves
125 g (4 oz) taleggio cheese,
  chopped
2 tablespoons grated Parmesan
  cheese
salt and pepper

- Heat the olive oil in a saucepan and sauté the spring onions for 1 minute.

- Stir in the sweetcorn, then pour in the vegetable stock and bring to the boil.

- Pour in the polenta and cook, stirring constantly, for 1 minute, until the polenta thickens.

- Stir in the spinach and cheese and season with salt and pepper. Serve drizzled with a little olive oil.

---

2 Sweetcorn and Tuna Pasta Salad

Cook 300 g (10 oz) farfalle in a saucepan of boiling water according to the packet instructions, until 'al dente'. Drain, refresh under cold water and place in a large bowl. Heat 2 tablespoons olive oil in a frying pan and cook 2 x 125 g (4 oz) tuna steaks for 2–3 minutes on each side. Leave to rest for 1–2 minutes, then break into chunks and add to the pasta with 100 g (3½ oz) roasted red peppers from a jar, drained and sliced, ½ thickly sliced cucumber, 400 g (13 oz) drained canned sweetcorn and 30 g (1¼ oz) rocket leaves. Whisk together 3 tablespoons extra virgin olive oil, the juice of ½ lemon, ½ teaspoon wholegrain mustard and 1 teaspoon honey in a small bowl, then toss with the salad and serve.

3 Sweetcorn and Potato Soup

Heat 2 tablespoons olive oil in a saucepan and sauté 1 chopped onion and 1 crushed garlic clove. Add 300 g (10 oz) chopped potato and cook for a further 3–4 minutes. Add 400 g (13 oz) frozen sweetcorn and cook for 2 minutes, then pour in 1.2 litres (2 pints) vegetable stock. Bring to the boil and then simmer for 8–10 minutes, until the potato is tender. Stir in 100 ml (3½ fl oz) double cream. Using a hand blender, or in a food processor or blender, blend the soup until smooth. Season well and serve garnished with chopped chives.

ITA-PIZZ-VAN

Rigatoni with Mussels and Courgettes

Serves 4

1.5 kg (3 lb) mussels, cleaned
200 ml (7 fl oz) white wine
400 g (13 oz) rigatoni
2 tablespoons olive oil
1 onion, diced
2 garlic cloves, crushed
2 courgettes, sliced

To serve

3 tablespoons grated Parmesan cheese
2 tablespoons chopped chives

- Place the mussels and wine in a large saucepan and cook over a high heat for 5–6 minutes, until the mussels open. Drain, reserving the cooking liquid, and remove the mussels from their shells. Discard any mussels that have not opened.

- Cook the rigatoni in a saucepan of boiling water according to the packet instructions, until 'al dente'.

- Meanwhile, heat the olive oil in a saucepan and sauté the onion and garlic for 2–3 minutes, then add the courgettes and cook for a further 4–5 minutes.

- Drain the pasta and stir into the courgettes with the mussels and strained mussel cooking liquid.

- Serve sprinkled with grated Parmesan and chopped chives.

Rigatoni, Mussel and Feta Salad

Cook 350 g (11½ oz) rigatoni in a saucepan according to the packet instructions, until 'al dente', adding 150 g (5 oz) frozen peas 1 minute before the end of cooking. Meanwhile, mix together 200 g (7 oz) crumbled feta, with 50 g (2 oz) rocket, the grated rind of 1 lemon, 1 grated courgette, 2 tablespoons chopped mint and 20 smoked mussels. Drain the pasta and peas and refresh under cold water. Toss with the other ingredients and add 2 tablespoons extra-virgin olive oil and the juice of ½ lemon. Season and serve.

Mussel and Courgette Fritters

Roughly chop 250 g (8 oz) pack ready-cooked mussels (smoked mussels can also be used). Put in a bowl, add 3 grated courgettes, 4 sliced spring onions and 3 tablespoons chopped coriander and mix together. Sift 125 g (4 oz) plain flour into another bowl, then whisk in 125 ml (4 fl oz) milk and 3 beaten eggs, until you have a smooth batter. Add in the mussel mixture. Heat 2 tablespoons olive oil in a frying pan, pour in 1 tablespoon of the batter and cook for 3–4 minutes on each side, until the fritter is golden brown. Mix together 200 g (7 oz) natural yogurt and 2 tablespoons chopped mint leaves and serve with the fritters.

ITA-PIZZ-BYL

Cheese and Spinach Calzones

Serves 4

500 g (1 lb) strong bread flour,
  plus extra for dusting
1 x 7-g (¼-oz) sachet dried yeast
a pinch of salt
3 tablespoons olive oil
300 ml (1 pint) warm water
300 g (10 oz) spinach
400 g (13 oz) ricotta cheese
4 tablespoons grated Parmesan
  cheese
4 tablespoons grated Pecorino
  cheese
4 spring onions, sliced
1 teaspoon freshly ground
  black pepper

• To make the dough, place the flour, yeast and salt in a large bowl and mix together. Make a well in the centre. Stir in 1 tablespoon of the olive oil and most of the measurement water. Mix together with your hand, gradually adding more water if necessary, until you have a soft, but not sticky dough.

• Turn the dough out on to a floured work surface and knead for 5–10 minutes until the dough is smooth and elastic. Divide into 4 pieces and roll out to 20 cm (8 inch) circles.

• Heat the remaining olive oil in a frying pan, add the spinach and cook for 2–3 minutes, until completely wilted. Place in a bowl and stir in the remaining ingredients.

• Divide the mixture between the 4 circles of dough, placing the mixture on to one half of each circle, leaving a 2.5 cm (1 inch) clean edge. Brush the clean edges with water and then fold the other half over the filling and pinch the edges together to seal. Place the calzones on a baking sheet and bake in a preheated oven, 220°C (425°F), Gas Mark 7, for 6–8 minutes, until the dough is cooked and the filling is hot.

1 **Cheese and Spinach Stuffed Pitta Breads** Heat 1 tablespoon olive oil in a frying pan and sauté 1 sliced red onion for a few minutes, then add 250 g (8 oz) spinach leaves and stir to wilt. Take off the heat and mix with 4 tablespoons grated Parmesan and 200 g (7 oz) torn mozzarella. Heat 4 pitta breads, slice along one side and open up. Fill each pitta with the spinach filling and top with slices of salami.

2 **Cheese and Spinach Pasta Salad** Toast 100 g (3½ oz) pine nuts in a dry frying pan, until golden. Cook 400 g (13 oz) fusilli in a saucepan of boiling water according to the packet instructions, until 'al dente'. Drain and refresh the pasta under cold running water and then toss with 2 tablespoons olive oil to prevent the pasta from sticking together. In a serving bowl, toss together 150 g (5 oz) baby spinach leaves with 200 g (7 oz) grated Cheddar cheese and 4 tablespoons grated Parmesan cheese. Stir in 4 sliced spring onions, 100 g (3½ oz) halved cherry tomatoes and the pasta. Whisk together 2 tablespoons olive oil and 1 tablespoon balsamic vinegar and pour over the salad. Serve sprinkled with the toasted pine nuts.

ITA-PIZZ-PAV

Spaghetti Puttanesca

Serves 4

1 tablespoon olive oil
4 garlic cloves, thinly sliced
2 x 400 g (13 oz) cans chopped
   tomatoes
2 tablespoons capers, chopped
4 anchovy fillets, chopped
a handful of green olives, pitted
   and sliced
1 teaspoon dried chilli flakes
a small handful of parsley,
   roughly chopped
400 g (13 oz) spaghetti

- Heat the olive oil in a saucepan and cook the garlic for 1 minute, then add the tomatoes, capers, anchovies, olives and chilli flakes. Simmer for 10 minutes, until the sauce starts to thicken. Stir in the chopped parsley.

- Meanwhile, cook the spaghetti in a saucepan of boiling water according to the packet instructions, until 'al dente'. Drain the pasta, toss in the sauce and serve.

Quick Green Bean and Anchovy Risotto Steam 400 g (13 oz) trimmed green beans for 6–7 minutes, until just tender. Meanwhile, boil 4 eggs for 4 minutes, then refresh under cold running water. Remove the shells. Whisk together 3 tablespoons extra virgin olive oil, 1 tablespoon sherry vinegar, 1 teaspoon Dijon mustard and a pinch of sugar in a small bowl. Heat a 400 g (13 oz) pack ready-cooked risotto of your choice according to the packet instructions until piping hot, then spoon on to 4 warmed plates or bowls. Divide the beans between the plates, then top each with a halved soft-boiled egg and 2–3 halved anchovy fillets. Drizzle with the dressing and serve.

Sicilian Anchovy Spaghetti Halve 6 plum tomatoes, put in a roasting tin and roast for 15 minutes in a preheated oven, 200°C (400°F), Gas Mark 6. Cook 350 g (11½ oz) spaghetti in a saucepan of boiling water according to the packet instructions, until 'al dente'. Meanwhile, heat 1 tablespoon olive oil in a frying pan and fry 3 eggs until the white is set but the yolk is still runny. Chop the tomatoes roughly and stir in 4 chopped anchovy fillets, 1 chopped garlic clove, 1 tablespoon chopped gherkins and 50 g (2 oz) breadcrumbs. Chop the eggs and add to the mixture. Drain the pasta and stir into the sauce with 1 tablespoon olive oil and 1 tablespoon chopped parsley. Serve immediately sprinkled with 2 tablespoons grated Parmesan cheese.

Aubergine and Courgette Ratatouille Pizzas

Serves 4

2 tablespoons olive oil

1 red onion, chopped

2 garlic cloves, crushed

1 large aubergine, cut into bite-sized pieces

3 courgettes, halved and sliced

1 red pepper, cored, deseeded and chopped

1 yellow pepper, cored, deseeded and chopped

400 g (13 oz) can chopped tomatoes

4 ready-made pizza bases

a small handful of basil leaves, torn

200 g (7 oz) mozzarella cheese, grated

- Heat the olive oil in a large frying pan and sauté the onion and garlic for 1–2 minutes. Add the aubergine and cook for 3–4 minutes, then add the courgettes and peppers, and cook over a low heat for 4–5 minutes.

- Stir in the chopped tomatoes, bring to a simmer and cook for 2–3 minutes, until the vegetables start to soften.

- Using a slotted spoon, divide the mixture between the pizza bases on 2 baking sheets. Top with the basil and grated mozzarella and bake in a preheated oven, 220°C (425°F), Gas Mark 7, for 11–13 minutes. Serve immediately.

---

10 Quick Aubergine and Courgette Pizzas

Toast 4 wholemeal pitta breads under a preheated hot grill for 1–2 minutes on each side. Spread each one with 1 tablespoon tomato ketchup. Top each with 1–2 pieces of shop-bought chargrilled aubergine, 1–2 pieces of roasted red pepper from a jar, 1 slice of shop-bought chargrilled courgette and 1 tablespoon grated mozzarella cheese. Cook under a preheated hot grill for 3–4 minutes, until the cheese is melted.

20 Rice, Courgette and Feta Salad

Cook 150 g (5 oz) basmati rice in a saucepan of boiling water according to the packet instructions, until tender, then drain and refresh under cold water. Slice 2 courgettes thinly with a vegetable peeler. Toss together the rice, courgettes, 4 sliced spring onions, 1 finely diced red chilli, 2 tablespoons drained and chopped marinated aubergine, 200 g (7 oz) crumbled feta cheese and 2 tablespoons chopped parsley. Drizzle over 2 tablespoons olive oil and 1 tablespoon white wine vinegar and gently toss together.

30 Pepperoni Pasta

Serves 4

350 g (11½ oz) spiral pasta
1 tablespoon olive oil
1 onion, chopped
2 red peppers, cored, deseeded
and chopped
350 g (11½ oz) minced beef
400 g (13 oz) can chopped
tomatoes
100 ml (3½ fl oz) red wine
125 g (4 oz) pepperoni sausage,
sliced
4 tablespoons grated Parmesan
cheese

- Cook the spiral pasta in a saucepan of boiling water according to the packet instructions, until 'al dente'.

- Meanwhile, heat the olive oil in a frying pan and sauté the onion and red pepper for 4–5 minutes. Stir in the minced beef and brown for 3–4 minutes.

- Pour in the chopped tomatoes, red wine and pepperoni, bring to the boil and simmer for 8–10 minutes.

- Drain the pasta and stir into the meat mixture. Pour into an ovenproof dish and sprinkle with the grated Parmesan.

- Cook under a preheated hot grill for 2–3 minutes, until the cheese is golden. Serve immediately.

10 Pepperoni Rice Salad

Heat 2 tablespoons olive oil in a frying pan and sauté 1 chopped onion for a few minutes, then stir in 150 g (5 oz) chopped pepperoni sausage and fry until a little crisp around the edges. Stir in 350 g (11½ oz) shop-bought ready-cooked rice, 2 tablespoons chopped sun-dried tomatoes and 150 g (5 oz) defrosted frozen peas. Serve sprinkled with chopped parsley.

20 Pepperoni Pizza

Place 4 ready-made pizza bases on to 2 baking sheets and spread each one with 100 g (3½ oz) passata. Top each one with 1 sliced tomato, 75 g (3 oz) sliced pepperoni and 50 g (2 oz) grated mozzarella cheese. Bake in a preheated oven, 220°C (425°F), Gas Mark 7, for 11–13 minutes, until the cheese is melted and golden.

Cheese Gnocchi with Spinach and Walnuts

Serves 4

1 tablespoon olive oil
250 g (8 oz) baby spinach leaves
500 g (1 lb) gnocchi
200 g (7 oz) crème fraîche
½ teaspoon wholegrain mustard
75 g (3 oz) Cheddar cheese, grated
25 g (1 oz) Pecorino cheese, grated
25 g (1 oz) walnut pieces

- Heat the olive oil in a frying pan and cook the spinach until it has wilted.

- Cook the gnocchi in a saucepan of boiling water according to the packet instructions. Drain.

- Place the crème fraîche and mustard in a saucepan and stir in roughly half of each of the cheeses and cook for 2–3 minutes, then stir in the spinach and gnocchi to heat through. Stir in the walnuts.

- Pour into an ovenproof dish and sprinkle with the remaining cheese. Cook under a preheated hot grill for 3–4 minutes, until golden and serve.

1 Cheese and Spinach Omelette

Whisk together 12 eggs in a bowl and season well. Heat 10 g (⅓ oz) butter and ½ tablespoon olive oil in an omelette pan or small frying pan and pour in one-quarter of the egg mixture. Move it around for 1 minute to allow all the egg to start cooking. When cooked underneath, sprinkle the omelette with a small handful of baby spinach leaves and 50 g (2 oz) Fontina cheese. Cook for 1–2 minutes then, using a palette knife, fold one half of the omelette over the other and slide on to a warm plate to serve. Repeat 3 more times with the remaining egg mixture and the same amount of spinach and Fontina cheese, to make 4 omelettes.

2 Cheesy Spinach Polenta with Creamy Mushrooms

Heat 2 tablespoons olive oil in a saucepan and sauté 200 g (7 oz) chopped chestnut mushrooms with 2 chopped shallots and 2 chopped garlic cloves. Stir in 3 tablespoons crème fraîche with ½ teaspoon wholegrain mustard and 25 g (1 oz) chopped toasted walnuts. Heat 1.3 litres (2¼ pints) boiling vegetable stock in another pan, pour in 275 g (9 oz) instant polenta and cook, stirring constantly, for 5–6 minutes, until thick and creamy. Remove from the heat and stir in 100 g (3½ oz) Fontina cheese and 50 g (2 oz) roughly chopped baby spinach leaves. Divide the polenta between 4 warmed bowls, spoon over the creamy mushrooms and serve sprinkled with 2 tablespoons grated Pecorino cheese.

ITA-PIZZ-GOQ

Margherita Pizza

Serves 4

1 kg (2 lb) strong bread flour, plus extra for dusting

2 x 7-g (¼-oz) sachets dried yeast

a pinch of salt

2 tablespoons olive oil

600 ml (1 pint) warm water

500 g (1 lb) passatta

6 plum tomatoes, sliced

450 g (14½ oz) mozzarella, sliced

- To make the dough, place the flour, yeast and salt in a large bowl and mix together. Make a well in the centre. Stir in 1 tablespoon of the olive oil and most of the measurement water.

- Mix together with your hand, gradually adding more water if necessary, until you have a soft but not sticky dough.

- Turn the dough out on to a floured work surface and knead for 5–10 minutes until the dough is smooth and elastic.

- Divide into 4 pieces and roll out to 30 cm (12 inch) circles, then place on pizza trays or baking sheets.

- Spread each one with passata, then cover with slices of tomato and dot with slices of mozzarella.

- Bake in a preheated oven, 220°C (425°F), Gas Mark 7, for 6–7 minutes, until the cheese is melted and golden. Serve immediately.

---

10 Super Speedy Tomato Pizzas

Toast 4 pitta breads on both sides under a preheated hot grill. Spread each with 1 tablespoon tomato ketchup and then cover with 4 sliced tomatoes. Top each one with 75 g (3 oz) grated or sliced mozzarella and cook under the hot grill, until the cheese is melted and golden. Serve sprinkled with chopped basil.

20 Spinach and Tomato Baked Eggs Steam 400 g (13 oz) spinach until wilted and drain well. Heat 1 tablespoon olive oil in a frying pan and cook 3 chopped tomatoes for 3–4 minutes. Stir in 2 tablespoons chopped basil leaves and season well. Add the wilted spinach and cook for 1–2 minutes. Divide the mixture between 4 ramekin

dishes and then break an egg into each one. Dot each dish with a knob of butter and bake in a preheated oven, 190°C (375°F), Gas Mark 5, for 10–12 minutes. Serve with toasted ciabatta.

Pea and Spring Onion Linguine

Serves 4

6 tablespoons olive oil

2 garlic cloves, chopped

a large handful of mint leaves

50 g (2 oz) toasted pine nuts

50 g (2 oz) Parmesan cheese, grated

350 g (11½ oz) linguine

225 g (7½ oz) fresh or frozen peas

4 spring onions, sliced

- Place the olive oil, garlic, mint, pine nuts and grated Parmesan in a blender or food processor and blend until smooth.

- Cook the linguini in a saucepan of boiling water according to the packet instructions, until 'al dente'.

- Meanwhile, cook the peas in a saucepan of boiling water for 3–4 minutes and then drain.

- Drain the pasta. Return to the pan and gently stir in the mint pesto, peas and spring onions. Serve immediately.

Spaghetti with Pea and Mint Pesto

Cook 400 g (13 oz) quick-cook spaghetti for 7–8 minutes, or according to the packet instructions, until 'al dente'. Meanwhile, blanch 250 g (8 oz) frozen peas in a saucepan of boiling water for 2 minutes, then drain and refresh under cold water. Place the peas in a food processor with 2 crushed garlic cloves, 50 g (2 oz) toasted pine nuts, 50 g (2 oz) grated Parmesan cheese, 6 tablespoons extra virgin olive oil, a small handful of mint leaves and some salt and pepper. Pulse briefly until roughly chopped, but not smooth. Drain the spaghetti, then return to the pan with the pesto and toss together well. Serve sprinkled with Parmesan cheese shavings.

Pea and Mint Tart

Dry-fry 125 g (4 oz) diced pancetta in a frying pan, until crisp. Add 2 finely chopped shallots and cook for a further 2–3 minutes. Spoon this into the base of a 23 cm (9 inch) shop-bought shortcrust pastry case. Beat together 4 large eggs and 300 ml (½ pint) double cream in a measuring jug. Stir in 225 g (7½ oz) defrosted frozen peas, 2 tablespoons chopped mint leaves and 50 g (2 oz) grated Gruyére cheese. Pour this into the pastry case, sprinkle with 2 tablespoons grated Parmesan cheese and cook in a preheated oven, 200°C (400°F), Gas Mark 6, for 20–22 minutes until golden. Serve warm or cold with salad.

ITA-PIZZ-TUH

QuickCook
Fish and
Seafood

Recipes listed by cooking time

10

Herb Butter Squid

Serves 4

125 g (4 oz) butter
grated rind of 1 lime and juice
   of ½ lime
2 tablespoons chopped mint
   leaves
2 tablespoons chopped basil
   leaves
1 tablespoon olive oil
500 g (1 lb) squid rings

- Mix together the butter, lime rind, mint and basil in a small bowl. Stir in the lime juice.

- Heat the olive oil in a large frying pan and cook the squid rings for 1–2 minutes on each side. Remove the squid from the pan and place them in a hot dish.

- Dot the squid with the herb butter and lightly toss together. Serve immediately.

2 Spiced Squid with Chickpeas

Place 450 g (14½ oz) squid, cleaned and cut into rings, in a non-metallic bowl and toss in the juice of 1 lime, 1 finely diced red chilli and 8 shredded basil leaves. Leave to marinate for 10 minutes. Place 1 shredded romaine lettuce and 150 g (5 oz) halved cherry tomatoes in a large salad bowl. Heat 2 tablespoons olive oil in a frying pan and sauté 1 thinly sliced red onion for 3–4 minutes. Add the squid and marinade and cook over a high heat for 2–3 minutes. Add a 400 g (13 oz) can chickpeas, drained, and stir to coat with the spicy oil. Pour everything over the salad leaves and gently toss together.

3 Crispy Squid

Place 200 g (7 oz) plain flour, 1 tablespoon pepper and a pinch each of salt and chilli powder into a freezer bag. Shake everything together and then add 500 g (1 lb) squid rings. Pour groundnut oil into a deep-fryer or large saucepan and heat to 180–190°C (350–375°F) or until a cube of bread browns in 30 seconds when dropped into the oil. Remove some of the squid from the flour and shake off the excess. Working in batches, gently drop into the hot oil and cook for 3–4 minutes, until crisp. Remove with a slotted spoon and drain on kitchen paper. Meanwhile, stir 2 crushed garlic cloves into 5 tablespoons mayonnaise in a bowl. Serve the squid with the garlic mayonnaise and wedges of lemon.

Griddled Swordfish with Salsa Verde

Serves 4

1½ teaspoons Dijon mustard

450 ml (¾ pint) extra-virgin olive oil

4 anchovy fillets, chopped

a handful each of parsley, basil, mint and tarragon

2 tablespoons capers

1 garlic clove, crushed

2 tablespoons olive oil

4 swordfish steaks, about 150 g (5 oz) each

juice of 1 lemon

salt and pepper

crisp green salad, to serve

• Whisk together the mustard and 250 ml (8 fl oz) of the extra-virgin olive oil in a bowl until they have emulsified. Stir in the anchovies.

• Chop the herbs and capers together and then add these to the oil mixture along with the crushed garlic. Gradually add more of the extra-virgin olive oil until the sauce has a spooning consistency.

• Heat a griddle pan until hot. Brush the swordfish steaks on both sides with the olive oil and season well. Griddle the steaks for 2–3 minutes on each side, or until cooked through but still very moist.

• Add the lemon juice to the salsa verde and serve spooned over the griddled fish with a crisp green salad.

---

10 Swordfish with Quick Salsa Verde Cook 4 x 150 g (5 oz) swordfish steaks under a preheated hot grill for 2–3 minutes on each side, until cooked through. Meanwhile, place 2 garlic cloves, a small handful of capers, a small handful of pickled gherkins, 4 anchovy fillets, 2 large handfuls of parsley, a handful of basil leaves, a handful of mint leaves, 1 tablespoon mustard, 3 tablespoons white wine vinegar, 8 tablespoons extra-virgin olive oil and some salt and pepper in a food processor or blender. Blend until fully mixed and serve with the swordfish.

30 Swordfish with a Smoky Tomato Sauce Whisk together 3 tablespoons extra-virgin olive oil, the juice of 1 lemon, leaves from 3 thyme sprigs and 2 teaspoons pepper in a bowl. Put 4 swordfish steaks in a shallow dish large enough for them to sit side-by-side. Pour over the marinade and leave for 20 minutes. Meanwhile, cut 12 tomatoes in half and place, cut side up, on a baking sheet. Sprinkle with 1 teaspoon smoked paprika, drizzle with 2 tablespoons olive oil and season well. Scatter over a small handful of thyme leaves. Cook under a preheated hot grill until the skins have blackened a little. Spoon the tomatoes and juices into a pan over a gentle heat. Add a small handful of basil leaves and lightly crush the tomatoes with the leaves. Add 1 tablespoon red wine vinegar, 1 teaspoon dark brown sugar and 40 g (1¾ oz) pitted black olives. Wilt 200 g (7 oz) baby spinach leaves in a separate pan and then drain well. Heat a griddle pan and cook the marinated swordfish for 2–3 minutes on each side. Serve on a bed of wilted spinach, with the smoky tomato sauce.

ITA-FISH-HEC

Stuffed Mussels

Serves 4

1–1.5 kg (2–3 lb) large mussels,
cleaned (about 48 mussels)
60 g (2¼ oz) breadcrumbs
50 g (2 oz) walnut pieces
200 g (7 oz) butter
6 garlic cloves, chopped
juice of 1 lemon
2 tablespoons grated
Parmesan cheese
2 tablespoons chopped tarragon
a small handful of parsley,
chopped

- Steam the mussels in a large, covered saucepan until they open, then drain. Discard any mussels that do not open. Break off the empty half of the shells and place the mussels on a baking tray.

- Place the breadcrumbs, walnuts, butter, garlic, lemon juice and grated Parmesan in a food processor and blitz until the mixture starts to come together. Add the herbs and blend until combined.

- Divide the herb mixture between the mussels, making sure each mussel is covered. Cook under a preheated hot grill for 2–3 minutes, until the stuffing is golden. You may need to cook the mussels in batches if you cannot fit them all on 1 baking tray.

- Serve immediately.

---

1 Smoked Mussel Bruschetta

Toast 8 slices of ciabatta on both sides, then rub each slice with a garlic clove. Roughly chop 200 g (7 oz) smoked mussels and mix with 2 roughly chopped tomatoes, 1 tablespoon chopped parsley and the juice of ½ lemon. Spoon the mussel mixture on to the toast and serve topped with a few rocket leaves.

2 Mussel and Tomato Linguine

Steam 1 kg (2 lb) cleaned mussels over 50 ml (2 fl oz) white wine in a large saucepan, until they have opened. Drain the mussels, reserving the cooking liquid, discarding any that do not open. Heat 4 tablespoons olive oil in a saucepan and sauté 1 finely chopped onion, 4 sliced garlic cloves and ¼ teaspoon dried chilli flakes. Add 450 g (14½ oz) halved cherry tomatoes and cook for 5 minutes. Meanwhile, cook 450 g (14½ oz) linguine in a saucepan of boiling water according to the packet instructions, until 'al dente'. Strain the mussel cooking liquid into the pan of tomatoes and add the mussels, 2 tablespoons chopped parsley and the drained linguine. Toss everything together, season to taste and serve.

Mackerel with Beetroot and Potato Salad

Serves 4

200 g (7 oz) baby new potatoes
2 tablespoons olive oil
4 spring onions, sliced
4 small, ready-cooked beetroot, thickly sliced
4 mackerel fillets
grated rind and juice of 1 lemon
½ teaspoon freshly ground black pepper
60 g (2¼ oz) watercress
2 tablespoons capers, roughly chopped
150 g (5 oz) natural yogurt
4 lemon wedges, to serve

- Cook the new potatoes in a saucepan of boiling water, until tender.

- Drain and toss the potatoes with the olive oil, spring onions and beetroot in a large bowl.

- Place the mackerel fillets, skin side down, on a baking sheet and squeeze over the lemon juice and season with the pepper. Cook under a preheated hot grill for 3–4 minutes on each side, until cooked through.

- Meanwhile, toss the watercress into the potato salad, and stir the capers and lemon rind into the yogurt in a small jug.

- Divide the salad between 4 plates and top each with 1 grilled mackerel fillet and a spoonful of yogurt dressing. Serve with lemon wedges.

Smoked Mackerel and Beetroot Pâté

Mix together 300 g (10 oz) skinned and flaked smoked mackerel, the juice of ½ lemon, 150 g (5 oz) cream cheese, 2 teaspoons horseradish sauce and some salt and pepper. Serve the pâté on slices of toasted ciabatta and top with grated ready-cooked fresh beetroot.

Smoked Mackerel and Beetroot

Risotto Put 2 small ready-cooked fresh beetroots in a food processor or blender and blend until smooth. Heat 1 tablespoon olive oil in a large frying pan and sauté 2 diced shallots for 2–3 minutes, until softened but not coloured. Stir in 400 g (13 oz) Arborio rice and continue to stir, until the edges of the grains look translucent. Pour in 100 ml (3½ fl oz) white wine and cook for 1–2 minutes, until it is absorbed. Add a ladle from 900 ml (1½ pints) hot vegetable stock and stir continuously, until it has all been absorbed. Repeat with the remaining stock, adding a ladle at a time, until the rice is 'al dente'. Stir in the beetroot purée, another 2 diced ready-cooked beetroots and 2 flaked smoked mackerel fillets. Serve sprinkled with chopped chives.

30 Italian Fish and Seafood Stew

Serves 4

3 tablespoons olive oil
1 onion, finely chopped
1 fennel bulb, finely chopped
2 garlic cloves, sliced
1 teaspoon fennel seeds
400 g (13 oz) can chopped
   tomatoes
250 g (8 oz) clams, cleaned
2 litres (3½ pints) fish stock
a pinch of saffron threads
250 g (8 oz) cooked king prawns
4 x 100 g (3½ oz) red mullet
   fillets
400 g (13 oz) monkfish fillet,
   cut into chunks
2 tablespoons chopped parsley,

- Heat 2 tablespoons of the olive oil in a large saucepan and sauté the onion, fennel, garlic and fennel seeds for 4–5 minutes.

- Stir in the chopped tomatoes and cook for a further 12–14 minutes, until the vegetables are tender.

- Meanwhile, heat the remaining olive oil in a saucepan and cook the clams, covered, for 2–3 minutes, until they have all opened. Discard any clams that do not open.

- Pour the stock and saffron into the tomato mixture and bring to the boil. Add the prawns, red mullet and monkfish and simmer for 5–6 minutes, until the fish is cooked through and the prawns turn pink. Add the cooked clams.

- Stir through the chopped parsley and serve immediately.

---

10 Seafood Salad

Whisk together 3 tablespoons extra-virgin olive oil, the juice of ½ lemon, 1 crushed garlic clove and 2 tablespoons chopped parsley. Toss together 300 g (10 oz) chilled ready-cooked mixed seafood with 1 thinly sliced fennel bulb and 200 g (7 oz) halved cherry tomatoes. Trim 2 chicory bulbs and divide the leaves between 4 plates. Toss together the seafood and dressing and spoon over the chicory leaves. Serve with warm ciabatta.

20 Seafood Pasta

Cook 300 g (10 oz) spaghetti in a saucepan of boiling water according to the packet instructions, until 'al dente'. Meanwhile, heat 1 tablespoon olive oil in a frying pan and sauté 1 chopped onion and 2 crushed garlic cloves for 2–3 minutes. Stir in 1 teaspoon smoked paprika, a 400 g (13 oz) can chopped tomatoes and 100 ml (3½ fl oz) vegetable stock. Bring to a simmer, add 225 g (7½ oz) chilled ready-cooked mixed seafood and cook for 3–4 minutes. Drain the pasta and add to the seafood sauce with 2 tablespoons chopped parsley. Serve immediately.

Tuna in Tomato and Caper Sauce

Serves 4

4 tablespoons olive oil

600 g (1¼ lb) fresh tuna, cut into bite-sized pieces

1 large onion, sliced

3 red peppers, cored, deseeded and sliced into rings

8 capers

125 ml (4 fl oz) white wine

400 g (13 oz) can chopped tomatoes

125 ml (4 fl oz) water

2 tablespoons chopped basil leaves

8 slices of ciabatta

lemon wedges, to serve

- Heat 2 tablespoons of the olive oil in a large frying pan and brown the tuna on all sides.

- Add the onion, red peppers, capers and white wine. Bubble to reduce the wine by half and then pour in the chopped tomatoes and measurement water. Simmer for 10–12 minutes. Stir in the basil.

- Toast the ciabatta on both sides, then place 2 slices on 4 plates and spoon over the tuna and sauce. Serve with lemon wedges.

1 Tuna and Caper Spaghetti

Cook 400 g (13 oz) spaghetti in a saucepan of boiling water according to the packet instructions, until 'al dente'. Meanwhile, mix together 1 finely diced red onion, 1 finely chopped red chilli, 2 crushed garlic cloves, 2 tablespoons capers, the juice of 1 lemon, 3 tablespoons olive oil, 2 tablespoons chopped parsley and a drained 185 g (6¼ oz) can tuna flakes. Drain the pasta and toss everything together to serve.

3 Tuna Rice Salad

Cook 200 g (7 oz) basmati rice in a saucepan of boiling water according to the packet instructions, until tender. Drain and refresh under cold water, then place in a large bowl. Stir in a drained 185 g (6¼ oz) can tuna flakes, 100 g (3½ oz) defrosted and blanched petit pois, 2 cored, deseeded and diced red peppers, 1 cored, deseeded and diced yellow pepper, 3 chopped tomatoes, 4 sliced spring onions, 2 tablespoons chopped parsley and 50 g (2 oz) sliced green olives. Sprinkle with the juice of 1 lemon and 3 tablespoons extra-virgin olive oil, season and mix well to serve.

Prawn and Cannellini Bean Salad

Serves 4

4 plum tomatoes

2 tablespoons olive oil

4 spring onions

1 red chilli, deseeded and sliced

2 garlic cloves, sliced

6–8 basil leaves, shredded

1 tablespoon balsamic vinegar

1 teaspoon caster sugar

400 g (13 oz) can cannellini beans, rinsed and drained

225 g (7½ oz) cooked peeled king prawns

1 tablespoon chopped parsley

1 romaine lettuce

salt and pepper

- Place the tomatoes in a bowl and pour over boiling water. Leave to stand for 1 minute, then drain and refresh under cold water. Peel off the skins and dice the tomatoes. Place in a large bowl.

- Heat the olive oil in a frying pan and sauté the spring onions, red chilli and garlic for 2–3 minutes. Turn off the heat and stir in the basil, letting it wilt in the remaining heat.

- Add the balsamic vinegar and sugar and stir until the sugar has dissolved. Season.

- Add the drained cannellini beans, prawns and chopped parsley to the diced tomatoes, then pour over the dressing and toss together.

- Place a few romaine lettuce leaves on 4 plates, then spoon in the salad.

Cannellini Beans with Tuna

Heat 3 tablespoons olive oil in a large frying pan and sauté 1 finely diced red onion and 2 crushed garlic cloves, until softened. Stir in a 400 g (13 oz) can cannellini beans, rinsed and drained. Cook for 2–3 minutes to infuse the flavours, then take off the heat and stir in 4 tablespoons chopped parsley and a drained 185g (6¼ oz) can tuna flakes. Season with salt and pepper and serve.

Prawn Kebabs and Garlic and Cannellini Beans

Mix 2 teaspoons honey, the juice of 1 lime and 1 crushed garlic clove together in a bowl. Pour over 350 g (11½ oz) cooked peeled tiger prawns and leave to marinate for 5 minutes. Remove the stalks from 100 g (3½ oz) small closed-cup mushrooms. Core and deseed 1 red pepper and chop it into medium-sized chunks and slice 1 courgette. Remove the prawns from the marinade and thread them on to skewers, alternating with the vegetables. Place the kebabs under a preheated hot grill or on a hot griddle and cook for 6–7 minutes, until the edges of the vegetables start to turn golden, brushing the prawns with the remaining marinade every few minutes. Meanwhile, make the 10-minute recipe on the left, omitting the tuna, and serve with the kebabs once cooked, or stuff the salad into pitta breads with shredded lettuce to accompany the kebabs.

Chilli Cod in Tomato Sauce

Serves 4

2 tablespoons olive oil
1 onion, diced
2 garlic cloves, crushed
¼ teaspoon dried chilli flakes
1 red pepper, cored, deseeded
  and thinly sliced
400 g (13 oz) can chopped
  tomatoes
100 ml (3½ fl oz) white wine
12 black olives, pitted and sliced
4 skinless cod loin fillets, about
  150 g (5 oz) each
steamed green beans, to serve
  (optional)

- Heat the olive oil in a large frying pan and sauté the onion, garlic and chilli flakes for 3–4 minutes. Add the red pepper and cook for a further 3–4 minutes.

- Pour in the chopped tomatoes, white wine and black olives and simmer for 8 minutes.

- Add the cod loin fillets to the pan and cook for 8–10 minutes, turning once if not covered by the liquid, until cooked through.

- Serve with steamed green beans, if liked.

---

10 **Pesto-Crusted Cod** Heat 1 tablespoon olive oil in a flameproof frying pan and cook 4 x 150 g (5 oz) cod fillets for 2–3 minutes. Mix together 4 tablespoons fresh breadcrumbs with ½ finely diced red chilli, 2 tablespoons ready-made pesto and 3 sliced spring onions. Spoon the breadcrumb mixture over the fish and press down lightly. Sprinkle with 1 tablespoon grated Parmesan cheese and cook under a preheated hot grill for 2–3 minutes, until golden and cooked through. Serve with a crisp green salad.

20 **Chilli and Lemon Cod** Slice 1 lemon and place a few slices on 4 pieces of greaseproof paper. Season 4 x 150 g (5 oz) cod fillets with 1 teaspoon dried chilli flakes, ¼ teaspoon smoked paprika and a pinch of cayenne pepper. Place the cod fillets on top of the lemon slices. Make a parcel with the greaseproof paper, leaving one end open to pour in 1 tablespoon white wine to each parcel. Seal the parcels and place in an ovenproof dish. Cook in a preheated oven, 200°C (400°F), Gas Mark 6, for 15 minutes until cooked through.

Remove the fish from the paper and serve with steamed green vegetables and any juices left in the parcels.

ITA-FISH-CAP

30 Monkfish Wrapped in Prosciutto with Lentils and Spinach

Serves 4

4 skinless monkfish fillets, about
150 g (5 oz) each
juice of 1 lemon
6–8 basil leaves, chopped,
plus extra to garnish
2 teaspoons freshly ground
black pepper
4 slices of prosciutto, halved
lengthways
4 tablespoons olive oil
2 shallots, diced
400 g (13 oz) can green lentils,
drained
200 g (7 oz) baby spinach leaves
2 tablespoons crème fraîche
salt

- Sprinkle the monkfish with half the lemon juice, basil and pepper. Wrap each fillet in 2 slices of prosciutto and chill for 10 minutes.

- Meanwhile, heat half the olive oil in a frying pan and sauté the shallots for 3–4 minutes. Stir in the lentils and cook for 2–3 minutes to heat through.

- Stir the spinach into the lentils, letting it wilt. Squeeze over the remaining lemon juice, stir in the crème fraîche and season.

- Heat the remaining olive oil in another frying pan and cook the wrapped monkfish for 6–8 minutes, turning over 2–3 times, until cooked through.

- Serve the wrapped monkfish on a bed of lentils and spinach, sprinkled with torn basil leaves.

---

10 Monkfish and Lentil Salad

Toss together 150 g (5 oz) baby spinach leaves with a drained 400 g (13 oz) can green lentils, 150 g (5 oz) halved cherry tomatoes and a few torn basil leaves in a salad bowl. Pan-fry 300 g (10 oz) cubed monkfish in 1 tablespoon olive oil. Whisk together 3 tablespoons extra-virgin olive oil, 1 tablespoon balsamic vinegar, a pinch of dried chilli flakes, 1 teaspoon sugar and 2 crushed garlic cloves. Add the monkfish to the salad, pour over the dressing, then toss together. Serve sprinkled with 2 tablespoons toasted walnut pieces.

20 Monkfish Fillets in a Smoky Tomato

Sauce Heat 2 tablespoons olive oil in a frying pan and sauté 2 finely diced shallots. Add 2 crushed garlic cloves, ½ teaspoon smoked paprika and 1 cored, deseeded and thinly sliced red pepper. Pour in a 400 g (13 oz) can chopped tomatoes and simmer for 5–6 minutes. Stir in 100 g (3½ oz) shredded spinach leaves and cook until wilted. Heat 1 tablespoon olive oil in another frying pan and cook 450 g (14½ oz) monkfish fillet, cut into 2.5 cm (1 inch) chunks, for 1–2 minutes on each side.

Transfer the monkfish to the tomato sauce and stir in gently. Stir in 2 tablespoons chopped parsley and serve on a bed of cooked green lentils.

Tuna with Cannellini Bean and Roasted Red Pepper

Serves 4

3 red peppers, halved, cored and deseeded
200 g (7 oz) can tuna in oil
½ teaspoon mustard
½ teaspoon honey
½ teaspoon balsamic vinegar
400 g (13 oz) can cannellini beans, rinsed and drained
1 red onion, finely sliced
65 g (2½ oz) cherry tomatoes, halved
parsley leaves, to garnish

- Cook the red peppers, cut side down, under a preheated hot grill, until the skins turn black. Place them in a large bowl, cover with clingfilm and leave until cool enough to handle, then peel away the blackened skin. Slice the peppers.

- Drain the oil from the tuna into a bowl and whisk in the mustard, honey and balsamic vinegar to taste.

- Using a fork, break up the tuna and divide between 4 plates. Add the strips of red pepper, drained cannellini beans, red onion and cherry tomatoes.

- Pour over the dressing and toss very briefly. Serve scattered with parsley leaves.

---

10 Bean, Red Pepper and Prawn Soup

Heat 1 tablespoon olive oil in a saucepan and sauté 1 chopped onion, 2 chopped garlic cloves, 2 cored, deseeded and chopped red peppers and 1 sliced carrot. Add 2 x 400 g (13 oz) cans cannellini beans, rinsed and drained, and 1 litre (1¾ pints) hot vegetable stock. Bring to the boil, then simmer for 3–4 minutes. Using a hand blender, or in a food processor or blender, blend the soup until smooth, then stir in 275 g (9 oz) cooked peeled prawns and cook for 1 minute until piping hot. Serve sprinkled with chopped basil leaves and a swirl of natural yogurt.

30 Seared Tuna with Broccoli, Bean and Red Pepper Salad

Steam 200 g (7 oz) broccoli florets until tender. Refresh under cold water. Whisk together 3 tablespoons extra-virgin olive oil, 1 tablespoon balsamic vinegar, ½ teaspoon honey, ½ teaspoon mustard and ½ teaspoon dried chilli flakes in a bowl. Mix together a 400 g (13 oz) can butter beans, rinsed and drained, 50 g (2 oz) sliced sun-dried tomatoes, 1 small diced red onion and 1 cored, deseeded and diced red pepper in a salad bowl. Toss in the broccoli and dressing and mix well. Heat 2 tablespoons olive oil in a frying pan and fry 4 x 125 g (4 oz) tuna steaks for 2–3 minutes on each side. Leave to rest for 2 minutes before serving with the salad, sprinkled with 2 tablespoons toasted pine nuts and drizzled with 2 tablespoons olive oil.

Baked Trout with Olives

Serves 4

4 trout, about 225 g (7½ oz)
   each, scaled
4 tablespoons flour
2 tablespoons olive oil
1 onion, sliced
30 g (1¼ oz) pimento-stuffed
   green olives
400 g (13 oz) tomatoes, chopped
juice of 1 lemon
1 tablespoon capers
2 tablespoons chopped parsley,
   to garnish

- Dust the trout with flour. Heat the olive oil in a frying pan and brown the trout for 2–3 minutes on each side. Place the fish in an ovenproof dish big enough for them to sit in a single layer.

- Add the onion and olives to the frying pan, sauté for 3–4 minutes and then spoon over the fish. Scatter over the chopped tomatoes, lemon juice and capers and bake in a preheated oven, 190°C (375°F), Gas Mark 5, for 15–18 minutes, until the fish is cooked through.

- Serve scattered with chopped parsley.

1 Smoked Trout Pâté

Place 350 g (11½ oz) flaked smoked trout, 200 g (7 oz) unsalted butter, the juice of 1 lemon, 1 tablespoon creamed horseradish and a pinch of cayenne pepper into a food processor or blender and blend until smooth. Stir in another 100 g (3½ oz) flaked smoked trout, with 1 tablespoon crème fraîche and 2 tablespoons chopped chives. Serve with toasted ciabatta slices.

2 Creamy Smoked Trout and Pea

Fusilli Cook 400 g (13 oz) fusilli in a saucepan of boiling water according to the packet instructions, until 'al dente'. Add 175 g (6 oz) frozen peas for the last minute of cooking. Meanwhile, mix together 1 tablespoon creamed horseradish and 4 tablespoons crème fraîche in a bowl. Flake 250 g (8 oz) smoked trout fillets in another bowl. Drain the pasta and peas, return to the pan and stir in the crème fraîche and trout. Season and serve with a green salad.

Sea Bass Fillets with Lentil Salad

Serves 4

4 tablespoons olive oil

400 g (13 oz) can lentils, drained

2 tablespoons chopped parsley

1 red pepper, cored, deseeded
  and diced

3 spring onions, sliced

1 pink grapefruit

4 sea bass fillets, about 150 g
  (5 oz) each

- Heat 2 tablespoons of the olive oil in a small saucepan over a medium heat. Add the lentils, parsley, red pepper and spring onions and cook for 2–3 minutes.

- Peel and segment the grapefruit over the pan to catch the juice, then mix the segments into the lentils.

- Heat the remaining olive oil in a frying pan and fry the sea bass fillets for 2–3 minutes on each side, until cooked through.

- Serve on a bed of lentils.

2 Sea Bass Fillets with Crushed Olive Potatoes Cook 550 g (1 lb 3oz) chopped new potatoes in a saucepan of boiling water until tender. Meanwhile, heat 2 tablespoons olive oil in a frying pan and cook 4 x 150 g (5 oz) sea bass fillets, skin side down first, for 3–4 minutes on each side, until cooked through. Drain the potatoes, add 100 g (3½ oz) halved cherry tomatoes, 100 g (3½ oz) chopped pitted black olives, 3 tablespoons olive oil and 1 tablespoon chopped parsley and crush everything together with a fork. Divide the potatoes between 4 plates and top each one with a sea bass fillet.

3 Sea Bass Carpaccio Slice a 450 g (14½ oz) skinless sea bass fillet very thinly, slightly on the diagonal, and place it in a shallow dish. Mix the juice of 1 pink grapefruit, 3 tablespoons olive oil, 3 finely sliced spring onions and some pepper together in a bowl, whisking to thicken. Pour the marinade over the slices of fish and leave to marinate for 25 minutes. Place the chopped leaves from 1 romaine heart on a serving dish and sprinkle with 2 peeled and segmented pink grapefuits. Spoon over the marinated fish and serve sprinkled with 1 tablespoon sesame seeds.

30 Saffron Scallops with Apple and Pistachio Purée

Serves 4

4 tablespoons olive oil
1 cinnamon stick
4 cloves
3 dessert apples, peeled, cored and chopped
200 g (7 oz) pistachio nuts, shelled
juice of ½ lemon
1 tablespoon sherry vinegar
1 tablespoon honey
a small pinch of saffron threads
12 scallops

- Heat 1 tablespoon olive oil in a saucepan and cook the cinnamon stick and cloves for 1–2 minutes. Add the chopped apples. Cook over a low heat for 4–5 minutes, until the apples are soft.

- Remove the spices and stir in half the pistachios and cook for a further 3–4 minutes. Spoon the mixture into a food processor or blender and process until smooth. Stir in the lemon juice. Set aside and keep the purée warm.

- Put the remaining pistachios in a food processor or blender and process until finely chopped. Stir in 2 tablespoons olive oil.

- Heat the sherry vinegar in a small saucepan and simmer until reduced to 1 teaspoon. Stir in the honey and saffron.

- Heat the remaining olive oil in a frying pan and sear the scallops for 1 minute on each side – do not overcook. Pour the saffron and honey glaze in the pan for the last 30 seconds.

- To serve, divide the apple and pistachio purée between 4 warmed shallow bowls. Top each one with 3 scallops, then drizzle the pistachio oil around them.

1 Scallop and Watercress Salad

Toss together 60 g (2¼ oz) each of rocket, spinach and watercress leaves and 1 thinly sliced apple and 2 tablespoons Italian salad dressing. Heat 2 tablespoons sunflower oil in a frying pan and fry 6 sage leaves until crisp. Heat together a knob of butter and 1 tablespoon olive oil and cook 12 scallops for 1 minute on each side. Arrange the scallops over the salad leaves, sprinkle with 1 tablespoon capers, 2 tablespoons chopped pistachio nuts and the crispy sage leaves and serve.

2 Bacon-Wrapped Scallops

Cut 6 streaky bacon rashers in half lengthways, then wrap around 12 scallops. Use a cocktail stick to secure. Drizzle the scallops with lemon juice and place on a baking sheet. Bake in a preheated oven, 190°C (375°F), Gas Mark 5, for 15 minutes. Meanwhile, place 2 grated apples, 2 grated carrots and ½ finely sliced white cabbage in a salad bowl and toss together with 2 tablespoons olive oil, 1 teaspoon honey and the juice of ½ lemon. Sprinkle with 1 tablespoon chopped pistachio nuts. Serve the scallops with the coleslaw.

ITA-FISH-LEH

Creamy Mussels with Pancetta

Serves 4

4 slices of crusty Italian bread
3 garlic cloves, 1 whole, 2 crushed
2 tablespoons olive oil
200 g (7 oz) pancetta, diced
1.5 kg (3 lb) mussels, cleaned
200 ml (7 fl oz) cider
3 tablespoons crème fraîche
1 tablespoon chopped tarragon
1 tablespoon chopped parsley

- Toast the slices of bread on both sides, then rub each slice with the whole garlic clove and place in a warmed shallow bowl.

- Heat the olive oil in a large saucepan and fry the pancetta for 2–3 minutes, until crisp. Remove from the pan with a slotted spoon.

- Add the mussels to the pan with the crushed garlic and cider. Cover and leave to steam for 3–4 minutes, or until the mussels have opened. Discard any that do not open.

- Remove the mussels with a slotted spoon and place in the warm bowls over the toast.

- Add the crème fraîche to the mussel juices and boil for 1–2 minutes. Add the herbs and the pancetta and warm through before pouring over the mussels and serving.

Asparagus with Mussel Sauce

For the sauce, place 100 g (3½ oz) shop-bought ready-cooked, shelled mussels and 2 crushed garlic cloves in a small saucepan with 150 ml (¼ pint) hot fish stock and simmer for 2 minutes. Add 300 ml (½ pint) double cream and 1 tablespoon chopped parsley and simmer for 4–5 minutes, until the sauce has thickened. Meanwhile, wrap 12 asparagus spears each in a slice of pancetta and drizzle with 2 tablespoons olive oil. Heat a griddle pan and cook the asparagus for 4–5 minutes, turning occasionally, until chargrilled on all sides. Serve drizzled with the mussel sauce.

Mussel and Saffron Risotto

Heat 25 g (1 oz) butter in a large saucepan and sauté 2 chopped shallots for 1 minute, then pour in 150 ml (¼ pint) white wine. Bring to a simmer, add 1 kg (2 lb) cleaned mussels, cover and cook for 2–3 minutes until the mussels have opened. Discard any that do not open. Strain the mussels, reserving the cooking liquid in a pan. Remove the mussels from their shells and set aside. Top up the reserved cooking liquid with fish stock to 1 litre (1¾ pints) and keep warm. Heat 25 g (1 oz) butter in a separate pan and sauté 2 chopped shallots for 2 minutes, then stir in 300 g (10 oz) Arborio rice. Pour in a ladle of the hot stock and add 2 pinches of saffron threads and cook, stirring continuously, until the liquid has all been absorbed. Repeat with the remaining hot stock, adding a ladle at a time, until the rice is 'al dente'. Stir in the reserved mussels and serve sprinkled with grated Parmesan cheese.

10 Prawn and Tomato Salad

Serves 4

500 g (1 lb) cooked peeled king prawns

3 large tomatoes, chopped

1 red pepper, cored, deseeded and chopped

4 spring onions, sliced

25 g (1 oz) rocket leaves

3 tablespoons extra-virgin olive oil

2 tablespoons red wine vinegar

½ teaspoon cumin seeds

- Toss together the king prawns with the tomatoes, red pepper, spring onions and rocket leaves in a serving bowl.

- Whisk together the olive oil, red wine vinegar and cumin seeds in a small bowl or jar.

- Pour the dressing over the salad and toss together to serve.

20 Prawns with Beef Tomato and

Mozzarella Slice 3 beef tomatoes and 2 courgettes and cook on a hot griddle pan or barbecue until charred on each side. Layer the tomatoes and courgettes on a large platter with 200 g (7 oz) sliced mozzarella cheese, 12 roughly torn basil leaves and 12 cooked peeled tiger prawns. Drizzle over 3 tablespoons extra-virgin olive oil and the juice of ½ lemon and leave to stand for 5 minutes. Serve sprinkled with 2 tablespoons toasted pine nuts.

30 Prawn-Stuffed Beef Tomatoes

Heat 1 tablespoon olive oil in a frying pan and fry 2 chopped garlic cloves, 2 sliced spring onions and 10 cooked peeled king prawns for 4–5 minutes. Mix in 100 g (3½ oz) fresh breadcrumbs and 2 tablespoons chopped parsley and season to taste. Halve 4 beef tomatoes horizontally and deseed, then place in a roasting tin. Spoon in the prawn mixture. Sprinkle with 2 tablespoons grated Parmesan cheese and bake in a preheated oven, 220°C (425°F), Gas Mark 7, for 18–20 minutes. Serve with a green salad.

Pan-Fried Red Mullet with Green Beans

Serves 4

300 g (10 oz) green beans
2 tablespoons olive oil
1 red onion, chopped
2 red peppers, cored, deseeded
 and sliced
4 red mullet fillets, about 150 g
 (5 oz) each
2 tablespoons hazelnuts, chopped
2 tablespoons chopped parsley

- Steam or cook the green beans in a saucepan of boiling water until tender. Drain.

- Meanwhile, heat 1 tablespoon of the olive oil in a frying pan and sauté the onion for 2–3 minutes, then add the red peppers and cook for a further 2–3 minutes.

- Heat the remaining olive oil in another frying pan and cook the red mullet fillets for 3–4 minutes on each side, until cooked through.

- Toss the steamed beans and the hazelnuts into the peppers, then take off the heat and add the chopped parsley.

- Serve the fillets on a bed of beans and peppers.

Red Mullet with Tomato and Herb Sauce Heat 1 tablespoon olive oil in a frying pan and cook 4 x 150 g (5 oz) red mullet fillets for 3 minutes on each side, pouring in the juice of 1 orange when the fish is turned over. Remove the fish from the pan and keep warm. Add 6 chopped plum tomatoes, 1 tablespoon chopped tarragon and 1 tablespoon chopped dill to the pan and simmer for 3–4 minutes. Serve the fish with the tomato sauce.

Pancetta-Wrapped Red Mullet with Crushed Potatoes Wrap 4 x 150 g (5 oz) red mullet fillets each in 2 slices of overlapping pancetta, with 2–3 basil leaves tucked inside each one. Cook 300 g (10 oz) potatoes in a saucepan of boiling water until tender. Drain, add 50 g (2 oz) chopped pitted black olives, 2 tablespoons olive oil and some salt and pepper and roughly crush the potatoes with a fork. Meanwhile, toss 350 g (11½ oz) asparagus tips in 1 tablespoon olive oil, fry for 4–5 minutes, until slightly charred, then remove and keep warm. Heat another 1 tablespoon olive oil in the frying pan and cook the pancetta-wrapped fish for 3–4 minutes on each side, until cooked through. Serve with the potatoes and asparagus.

Mixed Seafood Casserole

Serves 4

4 tablespoons olive oil
1 onion, diced
4 garlic cloves, crushed
100 ml (3½ fl oz) white wine
400 g (13 oz) can chopped
  tomatoes
200 ml (7 fl oz) fish stock
a pinch of saffron threads
400 g (13 oz) pack ready-cooked
  mixed seafood
2 tablespoons chopped parsley
crusty bread, to serve (optional)

• Heat the olive oil in a heavy-based saucepan and sauté the onion and garlic for 3–4 minutes. Pour in the white wine and boil for 2–3 minutes, then add the chopped tomatoes, fish stock and saffron.

• Bring to a simmer, stir in the mixed seafood and chopped parsley and cook for 5–6 minutes to heat through.

• Serve with crusty bread, if liked.

Mixed Seafood Salad

Mix together a 400 g (13 oz) pack ready-cooked mixed seafood with 1 cored, deseeded and diced red pepper, 1 cored, deseeded and diced yellow pepper, 4 sliced spring onions, 200 g (7 oz) halved cherry tomatoes and 50 g (2 oz) rocket leaves in a salad bowl. Toss with 2 tablespoons olive oil and the juice of 1 lemon. Serve with crusty bread.

Seafood Risotto

Heat 2 tablespoons olive oil in a saucepan and sauté 1 diced onion, 1 finely diced red chilli and 2 crushed garlic cloves for 2–3 minutes. Stir in 350 g (11½ oz) Arborio rice and 2 tablespoons tomato purée and cook for 1–2 minutes. Pour in 100 ml (3½ fl oz) white wine and cook for 1–2 minutes, until it is absorbed. Add a ladle from a saucepan containing about 1 litre (1¾ pints) hot fish stock and stir continuously, until it has all been absorbed. Repeat with the remaining hot stock, adding a ladle at a time, until the rice is 'al dente'. Stir in a 400 g (13 oz) pack ready-cooked mixed seafood and a small handful of chopped parsley and cook for 2–3 minutes, or until the seafood is heated through. Squeeze in the juice of ½ lemon and serve immediately.

ITA-FISH-QAP

Marinated Sardines

Serves 4

12 butterflied sardines
100 ml (3½ fl oz) olive oil
grated rind and juice of 1 lime
2 tablespoons chopped basil
   leaves
¼ teaspoon dried chilli flakes

To serve

lemon wedges
ciabatta bread or crunchy green
   salad (optional)

- Place the sardines in a shallow non-metallic dish.

- Whisk together the olive oil, lime juice, basil and chilli flakes in a small bowl or jar and pour over the sardines. Cover with clingfilm and chill for 20 minutes.

- Cook the sardine fillets under a preheated hot grill for 1–2 minutes on each side, until cooked through.

- Serve with lemon wedges and ciabatta bread or crunchy green salad, if liked.

1   Sardine and Tomato Bruschetta

Lightly toast 8 slices of ciabatta on both sides, then rub each slice with a garlic clove. Slice 3 tomatoes thinly and lay the slices on the toast. Place a few rocket leaves on each. Top the bruschetta with 2 drained 115 g (3¾ oz) cans sardines in oil. Drizzle with the oil from the cans and season with pepper.

2   Sardines with Butter Beans

Heat 2 tablespoons olive oil in a large frying pan and cook 8 sardines that have been dipped in seasoned flour, for 3 minutes on each side, until cooked through. Remove from the pan and keep warm. Add 1 tablespoon olive oil to the pan and fry 2 finely chopped garlic cloves for 1 minute, then add 100 ml (3½ fl oz) white wine and boil for 1 minute, scraping any sticky bits off the bottom of the pan. Add a 400 g (13 oz) can butter beans, rinsed and drained, 200 g (7 oz) cherry tomatoes and 3 tablespoons chopped parsley. Return the sardines to the pan, squeeze over the juice of 1 lemon and season. Serve with crusty bread to mop up the juices.

Tuna and Cannellini Bean Salad

Serves 4

410 g (13¼ oz) can tuna, drained
100 g (3½ oz) chopped tomatoes
30 g (1¼ oz) pitted black olives
1 x 400 g (13 oz) can cannellini
    beans, rinsed and drained
1 red onion, sliced
50 g (2 oz) rocket leaves
extra-virgin olive oil, to serve

- Place the tuna in a serving bowl and break it into chunks using a fork.

- Mix in the chopped tomatoes, black olives, cannellini beans, red onion and rocket leaves.

- Drizzle with olive oil and serve immediately.

2 Speedy Tuna and Green Bean Salad

Make the Green Bean Salad (see right). Gently stir in 410 g (13¼ oz) canned, drained tuna chunks.

3 Pan-Fried Tuna with Green Bean Salad

Place 4 x 150 g (5 oz) tuna steaks on a board and season both sides with pepper. Steam 450 g (14½ oz) green beans for 4–5 minutes. Meanwhile, whisk together 3 tablespoons extra-virgin olive oil, with the juice of 1 lemon and ½ teaspoon honey in a salad bowl. Stir in 50 g (2 oz) chopped sun-dried tomatoes and 40 g (1¾ oz) pitted and sliced black olives. Toss the warm steamed beans in the dressing. Toast 65 g (2½ oz) hazelnuts in a dry frying pan, until golden, then roughly chop them and toss into the beans. Heat 1 tablespoon olive oil in a frying pan and cook the tuna for 3–4 minutes on each side, depending on how rare you like your tuna. Serve the pan-fried tuna on a bed of the bean salad.

QuickCook

Meat and Poultry

Recipes listed by cooking time

30

20

Lamb and Olive Stew

Serves 4

450 g (14½ oz) shoulder of lamb, cut into small cubes

2 tablespoons flour, seasoned

2 tablespoons olive oil

1 onion, chopped

2 carrots, diced

2 garlic cloves, chopped

½ tablespoon chopped rosemary

200 ml (7 fl oz) white wine

400 g (13 oz) can chopped tomatoes

12 black olives, pitted

grated rind and juice of 1 lemon

2 tablespoons chopped parsley

800 ml (1¼ pints) water

200 g (7 oz) instant polenta

25 g (1 oz) butter

2 tablespoons grated Parmesan cheese

- Dust the cubes of lamb with the seasoned flour. Heat the olive oil in a saucepan and brown the meat all over.

- Add the onions and cook for 3–4 minutes, stirring, then add the carrots, garlic and rosemary. Cook for 3–4 minutes.

- Pour in the white wine and chopped tomatoes, bring to the boil and then simmer for 20 minutes, until the lamb is tender.

- Stir in the olives, lemon rind and juice and chopped parsley 1 minute before the end of cooking.

- Meanwhile, bring the measurement water to boil in another saucepan and pour in the polenta. Cook, stirring constantly, for 1 minute. Stir in the butter and grated Parmesan and divide between 4 bowls.

- Spoon the lamb stew over the polenta and serve.

---

1 **Lamb Cutlets with Fried Polenta** Heat 2 tablespoons olive oil in a frying pan and fry 8 slices of ready-made polenta for 2 minutes on each side. Remove and keep warm. Add 1 tablespoon olive oil to the same pan and fry 1 finely diced onion and 1 finely diced red chilli for 1 minute before adding 8 lamb cutlets and a sprinkling of dried oregano. Cook the lamb for 2 minutes on each side. Sprinkle in a dash of red wine and 2 tablespoons chopped black olives. Serve the cutlets with the fried polenta.

2 **Rack of Lamb with Rosemary and Olives** Heat 1 tablespoon olive oil in a frying pan and brown 2 x 750 g–1 kg (1 lb 10 oz –2 lb) racks of lamb. Place them both in a roasting tin and pour over 300 ml (½ pint) white wine, 2–3 rosemary sprigs, 30 pitted black olives and 3 tablespoons capers. Cook in a preheated oven, 200°C (400°F), Gas Mark 6, for 15 minutes. Meanwhile, steam 200 g (7 oz) broccoli florets and 2 sliced courgettes. Serve the lamb carved into cutlets with the juices from the tin and a side dish of steamed green vegetables.

 **Beef Carpaccio**

Serves 4

1 beef fillet, about 250 g (8 oz)

3 tablespoons extra-virgin olive oil

1 teaspoon freshly ground black pepper

1 tablespoon chopped thyme leaves

1 teaspoon Dijon mustard

½ tablespoon balsamic vinegar

½ teaspoon honey

60 g (2¼ oz) rocket leaves

25 g (1 oz) Parmesan cheese shavings, to serve

- Place the beef fillet on a chopping board and rub with 1 tablespoon of the olive oil, the pepper and thyme. Wrap in clingfilm and place in the freezer for 20 minutes.

- Meanwhile, whisk together the remaining olive oil, mustard, balsamic vinegar and honey in a bowl. Arrange the rocket on a serving plate.

- Unwrap the beef fillet, slice it as thinly as possible and then arrange over the rocket leaves.

- Serve sprinkled with Parmesan shavings and drizzled with the dressing.

 Steak Sandwich

Rub 450 g (14½ oz) rump steak with olive oil and season with pepper. Heat a griddle pan until very hot and cook the steak for 3–4 minutes on each side. Leave to rest. Meanwhile, cook 1 sliced red onion on a griddle for 1–2 minutes, then toast the cut sides of 4 opened ciabatta rolls on the griddle. Spread the roll bases with 1 tablespoon mayonnaise mixed with 1 teaspoon wholegrain mustard and then top with a small bunch of watercress and the cooked onion. Slice the steak and place on top. Top with the other half of the ciabatta rolls and serve.

Griddled Beef Salad

Whisk together 3 tablespoons extra-virgin olive oil, 1 tablespoon balsamic vinegar, ½ teaspoon creamed horseradish and ½ teaspoon honey in a small bowl. Heat a griddle pan or barbecue and cook 450 g (14½ oz) rump steak, until cooked to your liking. Leave to rest. Toss together 75 g (3 oz) mixed salad leaves, 2 thinly sliced and halved beef tomatoes, 2 sliced avocados and 1 cored, deseeded and sliced yellow pepper in a bowl. Divide the salad between 4 plates. Slice the steak and arrange on top of the salad. Drizzle over the horseradish dressing to serve.

Chicken Parmesan

Serves 4

4 boneless, skinless chicken
  breasts, about 150 g (5 oz) each
2 tablespoons plain flour
2 eggs, beaten
100 g (3½ oz) fresh breadcrumbs
75 g (3 oz) Parmesan cheese,
  grated
3 tablespoons olive oil
1 onion, diced
2 garlic cloves, crushed
400 g (13 oz) can chopped
  tomatoes
1 teaspoon dried oregano
¼ teaspoon dried chilli flakes
8–10 basil leaves, shredded
200 g (7 oz) mozzarella cheese,
  sliced

- Place each chicken breast between 2 pieces of clingfilm and, using a meat mallet or rolling pin, flatten each one to an even thickness of about 1 cm (½ inch).

- Place the flour in one shallow bowl, the eggs in another and the breadcrumbs and Parmesan mixed together in a third.

- Dip each chicken breast firstly in the flour, then the egg and finally the breadcrumb and Parmesan mixture so that it is completely coated. Chill for a few minutes.

- Heat 1 tablespoon of the olive oil in a frying pan and sauté the onion and garlic for 2–3 minutes. Add the chopped tomatoes, oregano and chilli flakes and simmer for 10 minutes.

- Meanwhile, heat the remaining olive oil in another frying pan and cook the chicken breasts for 4–5 minutes on each side, until golden.

- Pour the tomato sauce into an ovenproof dish. Place the chicken on top and sprinkle with the basil. Top each one with slices of mozzarella and bake in a preheated oven, 200°C (400°F), Gas Mark 6, for 10 minutes, or until the mozzarella is melted and golden and the chicken cooked through.

---

1 Quick Chicken Salad

Roughly shred 3 shop-bought ready-cooked chicken breasts. Mix in a bowl with 2 sliced mangoes, 50 g (2 oz) watercress and 100 g (3½ oz) Fontina cheese, roughly chopped. Whisk together 3 tablespoons olive oil, 1 tablespoon balsamic vinegar and ½ teaspoon mustard. Pour over the salad and sprinkle with 2 tablespoons toasted pumpkin seeds to serve.

2 Chicken and Parmesan Soup

Heat 1 tablespoon olive oil in a saucepan and add 1 diced onion, 2 crushed garlic cloves and 2 diced boneless, skinless chicken breasts. Cook for 5–6 minutes, stirring occasionally. Pour in 750 ml (1¼ pints) chicken stock, 100 ml (3½ fl oz) white wine and a 400 g (13 oz) can chopped tomatoes. Bring to a simmer and cook for 12 minutes. Stir in

3 tablespoons grated Parmesan cheese and 2 tablespoons shredded basil leaves. Serve with crusty bread.

Veal with Prosciutto and Sage

Serves 4

4 veal escalopes, about 150 g
  (5 oz) each
4 slices of prosciutto
4 sage leaves
2 tablespoons flour
3 tablespoons olive oil
350 g (11½ oz) green beans
grated rind of 1 lemon
25 g (1 oz) butter
100 ml (3½ oz) white wine
salt and pepper

- Place each veal escalope between 2 pieces of clingfilm and, using a meat mallet or rolling pin, flatten each one to an even thickness of about 5 mm (¼ inch).

- Place a slice of prosciutto and a sage leaf on top of each escalope and fix in place with a cocktail stick.

- Place the flour on a plate and season well. Toss each escalope in the seasoned flour.

- Steam the green beans and toss in 1 tablespoon of the olive oil and the lemon rind and keep warm.

- Heat the butter and the remaining olive oil in a frying pan and cook the escalopes for 2–3 minutes on each side.

- Remove the escalopes from the pan and pour in the wine, scraping all the sticky bits from the bottom of the pan. Boil for 1–2 minutes.

- Serve the escalopes on a bed of green beans with the sauce poured over.

---

10 Green Bean and Prosciutto Salad

Steam 450 g (14½ oz) green beans and fry 8 slices of prosciutto in 1 tablespoon olive oil, until crisp. Gently toss together the steamed green beans, 2 chopped avocados, 100 g (3½ oz) halved cherry tomatoes, 2 tablespoons toasted pine nuts and 200 g (7 oz) torn mozzarella cheese. Drizzle with 3 tablespoons olive oil and the juice of ½ lemon and then top with the roughly chopped crisp prosciutto.

30 Creamy Veal with Tagliatelle and Crisp Prosciutto

Cook 400 g (13 oz) tagliatelle in a saucepan of boiling water according to the packet instructions, until 'al dente'. Meanwhile, cut 400 g (13 oz) veal escalopes into strips and coat with seasoned flour. Heat 2 tablespoons olive oil in a frying pan and cook the veal for 6–7 minutes, until browned. Remove from the pan and keep warm. Add 1 chopped onion to the frying pan and sauté until golden, about 10 minutes. Pour in 100 ml (3½ fl oz) white wine and simmer for 4–5 minutes before adding 250 ml (8 fl oz) single cream, 2–3 tablespoons chicken stock and 2 skinned, deseeded and chopped tomatoes. Meanwhile, cook 8 slices of prosciutto under a preheated hot grill for 3–4 minutes on each side, until crisp. Return the veal to the pan with the drained pasta and 2 tablespoons chopped parsley. Toss together and serve topped with the crisp prosciutto and sprinkled with 2 tablespoons grated Parmesan cheese.

Lemon and Rosemary Pork with Cannellini Bean Salad

Serves 4

1 tablespoon olive oil

2 teaspoons finely chopped rosemary

4 garlic cloves, crushed

grated rind and juice of 1 lemon

4 boneless pork steaks, about 150 g (5 oz) each

1 red onion, sliced

2 tablespoons sherry vinegar

2 x 400 g (13 oz) cans cannellini beans, drained and rinsed

110 g (3¾ oz) mixed salad leaves

- Mix together the olive oil, rosemary, garlic and lemon juice in a non-metallic bowl. Add the pork steaks and toss in the oil to coat. Leave to stand for 10 minutes.

- Heat a griddle pan and cook the pork steaks for 3–4 minutes on each side, until cooked through. Remove from the pan and keep warm.

- Pour the remainder of the marinade into the pan, add the onion and cook for 2–3 minutes, then pour in the sherry vinegar and boil for 1–2 minutes.

- Stir in the drained cannellini beans and heat through.

- Toss the beans with the salad leaves and serve with the pork.

---

1 **Pancetta and Cannellini Bean Salad** Heat 2 tablespoons olive oil in a frying pan and sauté 1 sliced red onion, 125 g (4 oz) diced pancetta and 2 crushed garlic cloves for 2–3 minutes. Add 1 cored, deseeded and diced red pepper and cook for a further 1 minute. Pour in 2 x 400 g (13 oz) cans drained and rinsed cannellini beans and cook for 1–2 minutes to heat through. Stir in 2 tablespoons shredded basil leaves, some salt and pepper and the juice of ½ lemon to serve.

2 **Parmesan Pork Steaks with Cannellini Beans** Lay 4 x 175 g (6 oz) pork steaks between 2 pieces of clingfilm and, using a meat mallet or rolling pin, flatten each one to an even thickness of about 1 cm (½ inch). Mix together 25 g (1 oz) fresh breadcrumbs, a small handful of chopped sage and 2 tablespoons grated Parmesan cheese in a shallow dish. Put 1 beaten egg in another shallow dish. Dip each pork steak firstly into the egg and then into the breadcrumb mixture to coat.

Heat 2 tablespoons olive oil in a frying pan and fry the steaks for 3–4 minutes on each side, until golden. Meanwhile, heat a 400 g (13 oz) can cannellini beans, rinsed and drained, in a small saucepan, then stir in 1 tablespoon olive oil and 1 tablespoon chopped parsley. Serve the pork steaks with the beans and steamed cabbage.

Lamb-Stuffed Pittas

Serves 4

25 g (1 oz) rocket leaves
20 green olives, pitted and sliced
2 red peppers, cored, deseeded
  and sliced
2 avocados, stoned and chopped
2 tomatoes, chopped
4 spring onions, sliced
1 tablespoon Italian salad dressing
4 pitta breads
300 g (10 oz) leftover or
  shop-bought ready-cooked
  lamb, sliced

- Mix together the rocket leaves, olives, red peppers, avocados, tomatoes and spring onions in a bowl.

- Toss in the Italian salad dressing.

- Cook the pitta breads under a preheated hot grill for 1–2 minutes. While they are still warm, run a knife down one side and split them open to make 4 pockets.

- Divide the cooked lamb between each pitta and then spoon in the salad to serve.

---

2 Meat-Topped Pizzas

Heat 1 tablespoon olive oil in a frying pan and sauté 1 diced onion, 1 cored, deseeded and sliced red pepper and 2 crushed garlic cloves for 1–2 minutes. Stir in 400 g (13 oz) minced beef and brown the meat. Add a 400 g (13 oz) can chopped tomatoes and 2 tablespoons tomato purée and simmer for 3–4 minutes. Spoon the mixture over 4 ready-made pizza bases, sprinkle with 300 g (10 oz) grated mozzarella cheese and bake in a preheated oven, 220°C (425°F), Gas Mark 7, for 11–12 minutes, until golden.

3 Meat-Filled Calzones

To make the dough, place 500 g (1 lb) strong bread flour, a 7 g (¼ oz) sachet dried yeast and a pinch of salt in a large bowl and mix together. Make a well in the centre. Stir in 1 tablespoon olive oil and most of 300 ml (½ pint) warm water. Mix together with your hand, adding more water if necessary, until you have a soft, but not sticky dough. Turn out the dough on to a floured work surface and knead for 5–10 minutes, until the dough is smooth and elastic. Divide into 4 pieces and roll out to 20 cm (8 inch) circles. Mix together 150 g (5 oz) halved cherry tomatoes, 200 g (7 oz) chopped mozzarella cheese, 100 g (3½ oz) prosciutto, 100 g (3½ oz) salami, 1 tablespoon capers and 40 g (1¾ oz) grated Parmesan cheese in a bowl. Divide between the 4 circles of dough, placing the mixture on to one half of each circle and leaving a 2.5 cm (1 inch) clean edge. Brush the clean edges of the dough with water and then fold the other half over the filling and pinch the edges together to seal. Place the calzones on a large baking sheet and bake in a preheated oven, 220°C (425°F), Gas Mark 7, for 6–8 minutes, until the dough is cooked and the filling is hot.

Sage Liver and Mash

Serves 4

600 g (1¼ lb) shop-bought
  ready-made mashed potatoes
450 g (14½ oz) lambs' liver,
  sliced thinly
2 tablespoons flour, seasoned
50 g (2 oz) butter
4–5 sage leaves, chopped

- Heat the mashed potatoes according to the packet instructions.

- Meanwhile, dust the lambs' liver in the seasoned flour.

- Heat the butter in a frying pan and cook the liver with the sage leaves for 1–2 minutes on each side.

- Serve with the warmed mashed potatoes, pouring the butter and juices over the potatoes.

2 Lambs' Liver with Mushrooms

Dust 450 g (14½ oz) lambs' liver with 2 tablespoons plain flour seasoned with salt and pepper. Heat 1 tablespoon olive oil in a frying pan and cook the liver for 2 minutes on each side. Remove and keep warm. Heat another 1 tablespoon olive oil in a clean frying pan and sauté 1 sliced onion and 150 g (5 oz) sliced chestnut mushrooms for 4–5 minutes. Meanwhile, bring 800 ml (1¼ pints) water to the boil in a saucepan. Pour in 200 g (7 oz) instant polenta and cook for 1–2 minutes, stirring contantly, until it thickens. Prepare 1 tablespoon chopped chives and 1 tablespoon chopped parsley and stir half of these into the polenta. Add the remaining herbs to the mushroom mixture and then add the liver and the juice of 1 lemon and heat for 1 minute. Serve the liver and mushrooms spooned over the herb polenta.

3 Liver with Tomatoes and Pasta

Heat 1 tablespoon olive oil in a frying pan and sauté 1 sliced onion with 4 chopped streaky bacon rashers for 3–4 minutes. Add a 400 g (13 oz) can chopped tomatoes, 1 tablespoon Worcestershire sauce, 1 tablespoon tomato purée, ¼ teaspoon dried mixed herbs and 150 ml (¼ pint) vegetable stock. Bring to the boil and simmer for 12–15 minutes. Meanwhile, heat 50 g (2 oz) butter in another frying pan and cook 450 g (14½ oz) thinly sliced and floured lambs' liver for 1–2 minutes on each side. Cook 350 g (11½ oz) tagliatelle in a saucepan of boiling water according to the packet instructions, until 'al dente'. Drain and divide between 4 plates. Add the liver to the tomato sauce and serve poured over the pasta.

Quick Chicken Liver Salad

Serves 4

4 streaky bacon rashers
400 g (13 oz) chicken livers, trimmed
1 tablespoon extra-virgin olive oil
20 g (¾ oz) watercress
1 romaine lettuce, leaves torn
1 red onion, thinly sliced
salt and pepper
Italian salad dressing, to serve

- Cook the bacon rashers under a preheated hot grill until crisp. Leave to cool, then chop roughly.

- Meanwhile, season the chicken livers.

- Heat the olive oil in a frying pan and cook the chicken livers until golden but still pink in the middle. Leave to cool slightly, then cut into bite-sized pieces.

- Toss together the watercress, torn lettuce leaves and red onion in a large bowl.

- Add the chicken livers and chopped bacon, drizzle with Italian salad dressing and serve immediately.

Calves' Liver with Caramelized Onions Heat 2 tablespoons olive oil and 25 g (1 oz) butter in a frying pan and stir in 3 sliced large onions. Cook over a medium heat for 15 minutes, stirring frequently. Add a dash of balsamic vinegar and 1 tablespoon dark brown sugar and cook for a further 3–4 minutes. Meanwhile, heat 2 tablespoons olive oil and 30 g (1¼ oz) butter in another frying pan and cook 500 g (1 lb) calves' liver for 2–3 minutes on each side. Serve with the onions spooned over.

Calves' Liver with Sage and Mash Peel 875 g (1¾ lb) potatoes and cut them into equal-sized halves or quarters, depending on their size. Cook the potatoes in a saucepan of boiling water until tender. Heat 2 tablespoons olive oil and 30 g (1¼ oz) butter in a frying pan and fry 8–10 sage leaves until crispy. Remove from the pan and drain on kitchen paper. Drain the potatoes, mash them with 2 tablespoons crème fraîche and keep warm. Cook 500 g (1 lb) calves' liver in the same frying pan used for the sage for 2–3 minutes on each side. Meanwhile, heat another 2 tablespoons olive oil in a clean frying pan and cook 500 g (1 lb) baby spinach leaves until they start to wilt. Divide the mash between 4 plates, top with the wilted spinach and liver and finally the sage leaves. Pour over any juices from the pan and serve immediately.

Polenta-Crusted Pork with Pear and Rocket Salad

Serves 4

4 tablespoons instant polenta

4 tablespoons grated Parmesan cheese

2 tablespoons plain flour

1 egg, beaten

4 pork loin steaks, about 150 g (5 oz) each

3 pears, cored and sliced

1 red onion, sliced

75 g (3 oz) rocket leaves

2 tablespoons walnut pieces

3 tablespoons olive oil

1 tablespoon balsamic vinegar

50 g (2 oz) butter

- Mix together the polenta and Parmesan and place in a shallow bowl. Place the flour and egg in separate bowls.

- Dip the pork steaks into the flour, then the egg and finally coat with the polenta. Chill for 5 minutes.

- Place the pears, onion, rocket and walnuts in a bowl and toss with 2 tablespoons of the olive oil and the balsamic vinegar.

- Heat the remaining olive oil and butter in a frying pan and cook the pork steaks for 3–4 minutes on each side, until golden and cooked through.

- Serve on a bed of the dressed salad.

1 Pork Chops with Pan-Fried Polenta and Devilled Tomatoes

Sprinkle 4 halved large tomatoes with ½ teaspoon garam masala, 1 crushed garlic clove and some salt and pepper. Drizzle with 1 tablespoon olive oil and cook under a preheated hot grill for 4–5 minutes, until cooked. Meanwhile, heat 2 tablespoons olive oil in a large frying pan and cook 350 g (11½ oz) thick slices of ready-made polenta and 4 x 50 g (5 oz) pork loin chops for 3–4 minutes on each side, until golden and cooked through. Sprinkle with 1 tablespoon chopped basil leaves for the last minute of cooking. Serve the pork chops with the polenta, topped with the spiced tomatoes.

2 Pork Steaks with Pears

Heat 2 tablespoons olive oil in a roasting tin on the hob and cook 2 red onions cut into wedges, 2 cored and quartered pears and a few sprigs of rosemary. Add 4 x 150 g (5 oz) pork steaks and fry for 2–3 minutes on each side, until cooked through. Crumble over 60 g (2¼ oz) Gorgonzola cheese and place the roasting tin under a preheated hot grill and cook until the cheese starts to melt. Serve with steamed green vegetables.

30 Honey, Mustard and Lemon Lamb

Serves 4

4 garlic cloves, crushed
4 tablespoons honey
2 tablespoons wholegrain
  mustard
grated rind and juice of 1 lemon
a small handful of rosemary,
  chopped
2 tablespoons olive oil
4 lamb steaks, about 150 g
  (5 oz) each
300 g (10 oz) tagliatelle
1 red onion, sliced
2 courgettes, sliced

- Whisk together the garlic, honey, mustard, lemon rind and juice, rosemary and 1 tablespoon of the olive oil in a non-metallic bowl. Toss the lamb in the marinade and leave to stand for 10 minutes.

- Cook the tagliatelle in a saucepan of boiling water according to the packet instructions, until 'al dente'.

- Meanwhile, cook the lamb steaks under a preheated hot grill for 3–4 minutes on each side, or until cooked to your liking.

- Heat the remaining olive oil in a frying pan and sauté the onion and courgettes for 3–4 minutes, then pour in the remaining marinade. Simmer for 1–2 minutes.

- Drain the pasta and toss into the pan with the sliced onion and courgettes.

- Serve the lamb steaks with the tagliatelle.

10 Lamb and Asparagus Salad

Whisk together 3 tablespoons extra-virgin olive oil, 1 tablespoon lemon juice, ½ teaspoon wholegrain mustard and ½ teaspoon honey in a bowl. Toss 400 g (13 oz) asparagus tips in ½ tablespoon olive oil and cook on a hot griddle pan for 1–2 minutes. Place the asparagus on a bed of watercress, rocket and spinach leaves and top with 350 g (11½ oz) ready-cooked sliced lamb. Sprinkle with 200 g (7 oz) crumbled feta cheese and drizzle with the dressing to serve.

20 Italian Lamb Kebabs

Mix together 250 g (8 oz) minced lamb, ½ teaspoon fennel seeds, 1 crushed garlic clove, ½ tablespoon chopped basil leaves and salt and pepper in a large bowl. Divide the mixture into 8 balls, then thread 2 each on to 4 metal skewers and brush with oil. Cook on a preheated hot griddle pan for 8–10 minutes, turning until cooked all over. Serve with a crisp salad and a dressing made with 3 tablespoons extra-virgin olive oil, the juice of ½ lemon, ½ teaspoon Dijon mustard and ½ teaspoon honey.

ITA-MEAT-TEX

30 Roman Chicken with Peppers

Serves 4

3 tablespoons olive oil
4 boneless, skinless chicken
  breasts, about 150 g (5 oz) each
1 red onion, sliced
3 garlic cloves, crushed
2 red peppers, cored, deseeded
  and sliced
1 yellow pepper, cored, deseeded
  and sliced
1 green pepper, cored, deseeded
  and sliced
125 g (4 oz) green olives, pitted
400 g (13 oz) can cherry
  tomatoes
300 ml (½ pint) chicken stock
2 oregano sprigs
2 tablespoons chopped parsley
salt and pepper

- Heat the olive oil in a flameproof casserole and brown the chicken. Remove and set aside.

- Add the onion and garlic and sauté for 1–2 minutes. Add the peppers and cook for a further 2–3 minutes, then add the olives, cherry tomatoes, stock and oregano.

- Return the chicken to the casserole, bring to a simmer and cook for 20–22 minutes, covered, until the chicken is cooked through and tender.

- Stir in the chopped parsley, then season and serve.

---

10 Chicken and Pepper Salad

Toss together 2 cored, deseeded and sliced red peppers with 3 chopped tomatoes, 2 sliced avocados and a handful of baby spinach leaves in a salad bowl. Top with 3 shop-bought ready-cooked and sliced chicken breasts and 4 slices of pancetta that have been grilled until crisp. Drizzle with Italian salad dressing and serve with crusty bread.

20 Chicken and Red Pepper Panini

Halve, core and deseed 3 red peppers and cook, cut side down, under a preheated hot grill, until the skin turns black. Place in a bowl and cover with clingfilm until cool enough to peel away the blackened skin. Cut into strips. Meanwhile, mix together 4 tablespoons mayonnaise with 1 tablespoon pesto. Cut 2 ciabatta loaves in half horizontally and spread each cut side with the pesto mayonnaise. Place a small handful of baby spinach leaves and 200 g (7 oz) sliced mozzarella cheese on the bottom half of each loaf. Top with 3 shop-bought ready-cooked and sliced chicken breasts, 4 sliced tomatoes, the red pepper and a few basil leaves. Top with the other half of the loaf. Place both loaves on a hot griddle pan, pressing down with a heavy pan to flatten. Cook for about 3 minutes on each side, until the cheese starts to melt. Cut in half and serve hot.

Grilled Lamb with Anchovy Sauce

Serves 4

10–12 anchovy fillets
juice of 1 lemon
2 teaspoons chopped rosemary
4 tablespoons olive oil
8 lamb chops, about 150 g
  (5 oz) each
400 g (13 oz) tenderstem broccoli
pepper

- Place the anchovies in a pestle and mortar and pound them to a paste. Gradually add the lemon juice, followed by the rosemary and olive oil, until you have a creamy dressing. This can also be made in a food processor or blender.

- Season the lamb chops with pepper and cook under a preheated hot grill for 3–4 minutes on each side, or until cooked to your liking.

- Steam the broccoli for 3–4 minutes, until tender.

- Drizzle the lamb chops with the anchovy sauce and serve with the steamed broccoli.

10 Spaghetti with Lamb, Broccoli and Anchovies

Cook 350 g (11½ oz) spaghetti in a saucepan of boiling water according to the packet instructions, until 'al dente'. Add 350 g (11½ oz) broccoli florets for the last 3 minutes of cooking. Meanwhile, heat 3 tablespoons olive oil in a frying pan and cook 8 chopped anchovies and 1 finely chopped red chilli with 4 x 150 g (5 oz) sliced lamb loin chops for about 3–4 minutes. Add 100 g (3½ oz) breadcrumbs and cook, stirring, until the breadcrumbs are golden. Drain the spaghetti and broccoli and return to the pan with half the breadcrumb mixture and toss well with 2 tablespoons olive oil. Serve sprinkled with the remaining crumbs.

30 Lamb Caesar Salad with Anchovies

For the dressing, blend together 1 finely chopped garlic clove, 1 teaspoon Dijon mustard, ½ teaspoon Worcestershire sauce, 1 tablespoon lemon juice, 4 anchovy fillets, 3 tablespoons mayonnaise and 4 tablespoons natural yogurt. Toss 4 x 150 g (5 oz) sliced lamb loin fillets in 1 tablespoon olive oil, 2 teaspoons chopped thyme leaves, the juice of ½ lemon, 1 crushed garlic clove and some pepper. Cook on a preheated hot griddle pan for 5–6 minutes. Heat 2 tablespoons olive oil in a frying pan and cook 100 g (3½ oz) cubes of bread cut from a ciabatta loaf, until golden. Roughly tear the leaves of 2 cos lettuces and place in a large bowl or platter. Add the cooked lamb, 6 anchovy fillets and the croûtons. Spoon over the dressing and gently toss together before serving topped with 3 tablespoons Parmesan cheese shavings.

Meatballs with Tomato Sauce and Spaghetti

Serves 4

500 g (1 lb) minced beef
5 garlic cloves, crushed
¼ teaspoon dried oregano
1 tablespoon chopped parsley
2 tablespoons grated Parmesan
  cheese
2 tablespoons olive oil
1 onion, diced
a small pinch of dried chilli flakes
2 x 400 g (13 oz) can chopped
  tomatoes
100 ml (3½ fl oz) red wine
1 teaspoon sugar
2 tablespoons chopped basil
  leaves
375 g (12 oz) spaghetti
Parmesan cheese shavings,
  to serve

- Mix together the minced beef, 2 of the crushed garlic cloves, the oregano, chopped parsley and grated Parmesan in a mixing bowl. Roll into walnut-sized balls.

- Heat 1 tablespoon of the olive oil in a frying pan and fry the meatballs for 10–12 minutes, turning frequently.

- In another frying pan, heat the remaining olive oil and sauté the onion, remaining crushed garlic and chilli flakes for 3–4 minutes, then add the chopped tomatoes, red wine, sugar and basil and simmer for 8–10 minutes.

- Meanwhile, cook the spaghetti in a saucepan of boiling water according to the packet instructions, until 'al dente'.

- Transfer the meatballs to the tomato sauce and cook for a further 3–4 minutes, until cooked through.

- Drain the spaghetti and serve the meatballs spooned over the top. Serve sprinkled with Parmesan shavings.

 Quick Spaghetti Bolognese

Cook 400 g (13 oz) spaghetti according to packet instructions, until 'al dente'. Meanwhile, heat 1 tablespoon olive oil in a frying pan and sauté 1 diced red onion and 1 diced red chilli for 30 seconds. Stir in 300 g (10 oz) minced beef and cook over a high heat for 2–3 minutes. Stir in 400 ml (14 fl oz) Bolognese sauce from a jar and simmer for 3–4 minutes. Drain the pasta and divide between 4 bowls. Top with the sauce, 2 tablespoons shredded basil leaves and 2 tablespoons grated Parmesan.

Chicken 'Meat'balls

Heat 1 tablespoon olive oil in a frying pan and cook 400 g (13 oz) minced chicken with 50 g (2 oz) pine nuts for 5–6 minutes. Remove from the heat and place in a bowl with 1 tablespoon chopped basil leaves, 100 g (3½ oz) fresh breadcrumbs, 50 g (2 oz) grated Parmesan cheese, 2 beaten eggs and the grated rind and juice of 1 lemon. Use your hands to bring the mixture together, then divide into walnut-sized balls. Heat another 1 tablespoon olive oil in a frying pan and cook the meatballs, until brown all over and cooked through. Serve with 500 g (1 lb) ready-made warmed tomato sauce, sprinkled with chopped parsley.

 # Creamy Veal Escalopes

Serves 4

10 g (⅓ oz) dried porcini
4 veal escalopes, about 150 g
  (5 oz) each
2 tablespoons plain flour
50 g (2 oz) butter
1 tablespoon olive oil
2 garlic cloves, chopped
1 onion, chopped
100 g (3½ oz) chestnut
  mushrooms, sliced
100 ml (3½ fl oz) white wine
200 ml (7 fl oz) single cream
a large handful of baby spinach
  leaves
salt and pepper
mashed potatoes, to serve

- Soak the porcini in just enough boiling water to cover for 10 minutes. Drain, reserving the liquid, and roughly chop the porcini.

- Dust the veal escalopes with the flour. Heat the butter and the olive oil in a frying pan and cook the escalopes for 2–3 minutes on each side, until just cooked through. Remove from the pan and keep warm.

- Add the garlic, onion and mushrooms to the pan and sauté for 4–5 minutes, until the onion is soft.

- Pour in the wine and bubble for 2–3 minutes, then pour in the cream and 2–3 tablespoons of the reserved porcini liquid.

- Bring to the boil, then stir in the porcini and spinach and some salt and pepper. Return the escalopes to the pan and cook for 1 minute before serving with mashed potatoes.

1 Veal Salad

Heat 1 tablespoon olive oil in a frying pan and cook a 300 g (10 oz) veal steak for 1–2 minutes on each side, or until cooked to your liking. Rest for 1–2 minutes, then slice thinly against the grain. In a large salad bowl, toss the veal with 2 chopped beef tomatoes, 50 g (2 oz) bistro salad leaves, 20 g (¾ oz) rocket, 2 tablespoons chopped walnuts and 75 g (3 oz) sliced roasted peppers from a jar. Serve dressed with 2–3 tablespoons Italian salad dressing and sprinkled with 3 tablespoons Parmesan cheese shavings.

2 Veal Porcini with Pasta

Cook 350 g (11½ oz) pappardelle pasta in a saucepan of boiling water according to the packet instructions, until 'al dente'. Meanwhile, heat 2 tablespoons olive oil in a large frying pan and sauté 2 diced shallots and 1 crushed garlic clove. Add 275 g (9 oz) fresh porcini and 300 g (10 oz) thinly sliced veal and fry quickly over a high heat. Season well, stir in 150 ml (¼ pint) single cream and bring to a simmer. Drain the pasta and toss into the veal porcini sauce. Serve sprinkled with 2 tablespoons chopped parsley and 2 tablespoons grated Parmesan cheese.

10 Chicken BLT

Serves 4

4 back bacon rashers
8 wholemeal bread slices
2 teaspoons wholegrain mustard
4 crisp iceburg lettuce leaves
4 tomatoes, sliced
2 shop-bought ready-cooked
chicken breasts, sliced
1 avocado, stoned and sliced

- Fry the bacon rashers in a dry frying pan until crisp.

- Meanwhile, toast the wholemeal bread on both sides, then spread 4 slices with the wholegrain mustard.

- Place a lettuce leaf on each of these slices and top with the sliced tomato. Divide the chicken between the slices of toast.

- Top with the bacon and the avocado.

- Finish with the remaining slices of toast and, using cocktail sticks to keep the sandwiches together, cut on the diagonal to serve.

2 Warm Chicken Salad

Cut 4 x 150 g (5 oz) chicken breasts and 1 small baguette into chunks and place on a baking sheet. Sprinkle with 2 tablespoons olive oil and 2 crushed garlic cloves. Toss to coat and cook in a preheated oven, 200°C (400°F), Gas Mark 6, for 15 minutes, until the bread is crisp and the chicken is cooked through. Meanwhile, whisk together 3 tablespoons extra-virgin olive oil and 1 tablespoon balsamic vinegar. In a large bowl, toss together 175 g (6 oz) spinach leaves with 200 g (7 oz) halved cherry tomatoes and 200 g (7 oz) crumbled goats' cheese. Arrange the cooked chicken and bread in a serving dish and toss with the spinach salad. Drizzle with the dressing to serve.

3 Stuffed Chicken Breasts

Make a slit down the side of 4 x 150 g (5 oz) boneless, skinless chicken breasts to form a pocket. Stuff each pocket with 175 g (6 oz) sliced Fontina cheese and a handful of basil leaves. Wrap each chicken breast with 2 slices of Parma ham. Place on a baking sheet and cook in a preheated oven, 200°C (400°F), Gas Mark 6, for 20 minutes, until cooked through. Meanwhile, heat 2 tablespoons olive oil in a frying pan and toss in 250 g (8 oz) baby spinach leaves and 200 g (7 oz) cherry tomatoes. Cook briefly until the spinach starts to wilt. Serve the chicken breasts on a bed of wilted spinach.

Pork Escalopes with Peperonata

Serves 4

2 tablespoons olive oil

1 onion, finely diced

2 garlic cloves, crushed

2 red peppers, cored, deseeded and thinly sliced

1 yellow pepper, cored, deseeded and thinly sliced

2 tablespoons white wine

400 g (13 oz) can chopped tomatoes

4 pork escalopes, about 150 g (5 oz) each

1 tablespoon chopped oregano

purple sprouting broccoli, to serve

- Heat 1 tablespoon of the olive oil in a frying pan and sauté the onion for 3–4 minutes. Add the garlic and cook for a further 1 minute.

- Stir in the peppers and wine, bring to a simmer, cover and cook for 10 minutes.

- Pour in the chopped tomatoes and cook, uncovered, for a further 10–15 minutes, until the peppers are soft.

- Meanwhile, toss the pork escalopes in the remaining olive oil and the oregano and cook on a preheated hot griddle pan or barbecue for 3–4 minutes on each side.

- Serve the escalopes on a bed of the peperonata, with steamed purple sprouting broccoli.

 Pork Chops with Italian Purple Sprouting Broccoli Cook 650 g (1 lb 7 oz) purple sprouting broccoli in a saucepan of boiling water for 4–5 minutes. Drain. Meanwhile, dust 4 pork escalopes with seasoned flour. Heat 50 g (2 oz) butter and 1 tablespoon olive oil in a frying pan and cook the dusted escalopes with 2 teaspoons chopped sage leaves for 4–5 minutes, until cooked through. Heat 2 tablespoons olive oil in a frying pan, add the broccoli and cook for 1 minute. Add 2 chopped garlic cloves, ¼ teaspoon dried chilli flakes, the juice of ½ lemon and some pepper and cook for a further 1 minute. Serve with the pork.

Purple Sprouting Broccoli and Pancetta Soup Heat 2 tablespoons olive oil and sauté 200 g (7 oz) diced pancetta for 1–2 minutes. Remove half from the pan and then add 1 chopped onion and sauté for 2–3 minutes. Add 2 diced potatoes, 500 g (1 lb) purple sprouting broccoli and 900 ml (1½ pints) vegetable stock. Bring to the boil and simmer for 8–10 minutes, until the potato is tender. Stir in 200 g (7 oz) Gorgonzola cheese. Using a hand blender, or in a food processor or blender, blend the soup until smooth. Stir in 150 ml (¼ pint) milk, season and reheat gently before serving. Serve sprinkled with the remaining pancetta.

Lamb with Fennel and Marsala

Serves 4

3 tablespoons olive oil
2 fennel bulbs, thinly sliced
2 teaspoons chopped thyme
  leaves
50 ml (2 fl oz) marsala
100 ml (3½ fl oz) double cream
300 g (10 oz) frozen peas,
  defrosted
1 garlic clove, finely chopped
8 lamb cutlets, about 150 g
  (5 oz) each

- Heat 2 tablespoons of the olive oil in a frying pan and sauté the fennel and thyme for 1–2 minutes, until tender.

- Stir in the marsala, double cream and peas and simmer for 4–5 minutes.

- Heat the remaining oil in another pan and fry the garlic and lamb cutlets for 3–4 minutes on each side, until brown.

- Transfer the lamb cutlets to the vegetables and cook for a further 3–4 minutes, or until cooked to your liking.

10 Lamb Cutlets with Rosemary and Fennel

Steam 4 sliced fennel bulbs for 5–6 minutes until tender. Meanwhile, rub 8 lamb cutlets with a mixture of 1 tablespoon olive oil, 2 tablespoons chopped rosemary, 2 crushed garlic cloves and the grated rind of ½ lemon. Grill or fry the chops to your liking. Remove the fennel from the steamer and place in an ovenproof dish, sprinkle with the juice of ½ lemon, 3 tablespoons fresh breadcrumbs and 3 tablespoons grated Parmesan cheese. Cook under a preheated hot grill for 2–3 minutes until golden. Serve with the lamb.

30 Pesto-Crusted Rack of Lamb

Mix together 2 tablespoons ready-made pesto with 4 tablespoons fresh breadcrumbs in a bowl. Score the fat on 2 x 450 g (14½ oz) racks of lamb and spread the breadcrumb mixture over the fat, pressing it down. Cook in a preheated oven, 220°C (425°F), Gas Mark 7, for 14–16 minutes, or longer if you like your lamb less pink. Meanwhile, slice 3 fennel bulbs and toss in 2 tablespoons olive oil and the juice of ½ lemon. Season with pepper and cook on a hot griddle pan until caramelized. Serve the lamb racks with the griddled fennel and a watercress salad.

ITA-MEAT-DAZ

Sausage and Borlotti Bean Stew

Serves 4

2 tablespoons olive oil

4 Italian sausages, chopped

1 large onion, chopped

2 garlic cloves, chopped

1 teaspoon fennel seeds

2 x 400 g (13 oz) cans cherry
tomatoes

500 ml (17 fl oz) beef stock

2 x 400 g (13 oz) cans borlotti
beans, rinsed and drained

200 g (7 oz) green beans, halved

1 tablespoon chopped basil leaves

2 tablespoons grated Parmesan
cheese, to serve (optional)

- Heat the olive oil in a frying pan and brown the chunks of sausage for 3–4 minutes.

- Remove the sausage from the pan and add the onion, garlic and fennel seeds and cook for 3–4 minutes, then add the cherry tomatoes and stock.

- Bring to a simmer, return the sausages to the pan and add the borlotti beans.

- Cook for 10 minutes and then add the halved green beans and basil. Cook for a further 5–6 minutes until the sausages are cooked through and the beans are tender.

- Serve sprinkled with grated Parmesan, if liked.

Sausage Salad with Bean Dip

Toss together 50 g (2 oz) torn romaine lettuce leaves, 125 g (4 oz) roasted red peppers from a jar, drained and sliced, 2 tablespoons pitted black olives, 3 sliced tomatoes and 200 g (7 oz) thickly sliced ready-cooked Italian sausages in a salad bowl. Place a 400 g (13 oz) can borlotti beans, rinsed and drained, 2 crushed garlic cloves, the juice of ½ lemon, 2 tablespoons tahini and 4–5 tablespoons extra-virgin olive oil in a food processor or blender, then process until smooth, adding more oil if needed. Serve the salad with the dip, sprinkled with 1 tablespoon extra-virgin olive oil and 1 tablespoon toasted pine nuts.

Warm Sausage and Bean Salad

Cook 4 diagonally sliced Italian sausages under a preheated hot grill or on a hot barbecue for 3–4 minutes, until cooked through. Steam 350 g (11½ oz) green beans until tender and then refresh in cold water and drain. Toss together the sausages, beans, a 400 g (13 oz) can borlotti beans, drained and rinsed, 4 sliced tomatoes and 8–10 basil leaves in a large bowl. Whisk together 3 tablespoons olive oil, 1 tablespoon sherry vinegar, 1 crushed garlic clove, ½ teaspoon wholegrain mustard and ½ teaspoon honey in a separate bowl. Drizzle over the salad and serve with crusty bread.

Smoked Duck Breast Salad

Serves 4

2 oranges

2 tablespoons extra-virgin olive oil

½ teaspoon Dijon mustard

75 g (3 oz) watercress

a small handful of pomegranate seeds

250 g (8 oz) smoked duck breast, sliced

- Peel and segment the oranges over a bowl to catch the juice.

- Whisk the orange juice with the olive oil and Dijon mustard.

- Toss together the watercress, pomegranate seeds and orange segments in a bowl, then divide between 4 shallow bowls.

- Top with the smoked duck breast and drizzle with the dressing to serve.

20 Duck with Mushrooms and

Tagliatelle Heat 2 tablespoons olive oil in a frying pan and sauté 1 chopped red onion and 2 crushed garlic cloves for 1–2 minutes. Add 75 g (3 oz) sliced chestnut mushrooms and cook for a further 4–5 minutes. Stir in 100 ml (3½ fl oz) white wine, 2 teaspoons tomato purée, 300 g (10 oz) smoked sliced duck breast and 4 tablespoons crème fraîche and simmer for 5–6 minutes. Meanwhile, cook 350 g (11½ oz) tagliatelle in a saucepan of boiling water according to the packet instructions, until 'al dente'. Drain and toss with the smoked duck sauce. Serve sprinkled with 1 tablespoon thyme leaves.

30 Duck with Broccoli and Olives

Score the skin of 4 x 175 g (6 oz) duck breasts in a criss-cross pattern, with a sharp knife. Season the skin with salt and pepper. Heat an ovenproof frying pan and place the duck breasts skin side down in the pan. Cook for 7–8 minutes, until the fat runs out and the skin is golden. Turn the breasts over and brown on the other side. Remove 1–2 tablespoons of the duck fat and place in another frying pan. Transfer the duck pan to a preheated oven, 200°C (400°F), Gas Mark 6, and cook for 8–10 minutes, depending on how rare you like your duck. Meanwhile, steam 1 large head of broccoli, cut into florets, for 3–4 minutes. Heat the duck fat in the frying pan and sauté 2 diced shallots and 1 chopped red chilli for 3–4 minutes and then add the steamed broccoli, tossing to coat in the spicy oil. Sprinkle in 100 g (3½ oz) chopped pitted black olives. Remove the duck breasts from the oven and leave to rest for 5 minutes before serving with the broccoli.

QuickCook

Desserts and Cakes

Recipes listed by cooking time

30

20

10

Coconut Kisses

Serves 4

50 g (2 oz) unsalted butter,
  melted, plus extra for greasing
200 g (7 oz) desiccated coconut
50 g (2 oz) caster sugar
1 egg, beaten

- Grease a baking sheet. Place the coconut, sugar and melted butter in a bowl and mix together. Stir in the egg and mix well.

- Using your hands, take walnut-sized pieces of the mixture and shape them into little pyramids. Place on the prepared baking sheet and bake in a preheated oven, 150°C (300°F), Gas Mark 2, for 15 minutes, until golden.

- Leave to cool on a wire rack.

Coconut Dessert Sprinkle

Mix together ½ tablespoon olive oil, 1 tablespoon honey, 1 tablespoon maple syrup, 100 g (3½ oz) rolled oats, 25 g (1 oz) sunflower seeds, 2 tablespoons sesame seeds and 25 g (1 oz) flaked almonds in a bowl. Spread on to a baking sheet and cook under a preheated medium grill for 6–7 minutes, turning frequently, until golden. Pour into a large bowl and stir in 50 g (2 oz) dried cranberries and 25 g (1 oz) desiccated coconut. Serve with fresh fruit and yogurt.

Coconut Biscotti

Mix together 110 g (3¾ oz) caster sugar, 110 g (3¾ oz) plain flour, 1 teaspoon baking powder, the grated rind of 1 orange, 50 g (2 oz) blanched almonds, 15 g (½ oz) desiccated coconut and 1 egg in a bowl to make a stiff dough. Turn out on to a floured work surface and roll into a sausage shape about 28 cm (11 inches) long. Place on a baking sheet and bake in a preheated oven, 220°C (425°F), Gas mark 7, for 15 minutes. Remove from the oven, leave to cool for 2–3 minutes and then gently slice into biscotti. Lay the biscotti flat on the baking sheet and bake for a further 2–3 minutes to crisp. Leave to cool on a wire rack.

ITA-SWEE-VOU

Pear and Mascarpone Pancakes

Serves 4

125 g (4 oz) plain flour, sifted
2 eggs
300 ml (½ pint) milk
25 g (1 oz) butter, melted,
  plus extra for greasing
500 g (1 lb) mascarpone cheese
2 tablespoons Amaretto liqueur
3 ripe pears, peeled, cored
  and diced
4 tablespoons honey

- To make the pancake batter, place the flour in a large bowl and make a well in the centre. Pour the eggs into the centre and start to whisk, bringing in the flour. Gradually add the milk, whisking constantly until you have a batter the consistency of double cream. Whisk in the melted butter.

- Grease a frying pan with a little melted butter, using kitchen paper to take off any excess.

- Pour in a small amount of the batter, swirling it around to coat the base of the frying pan. Cook for 1–2 minutes and then flip the pancake over to cook the other side for about 1 minute. Repeat with the remaining batter to make 8 pancakes. Stack the pancakes between sheets of greaseproof paper wrapped in foil to keep warm.

- Meanwhile, whisk together the mascarpone and Amaretto in a bowl, then briefly fold in the diced pears and 2 tablespoons of the honey to make a rippled effect.

- Divide the mixture between the pancakes, fold each one into quarters and place in an ovenproof dish. Drizzle with the remaining honey and heat under a preheated hot grill for 1–2 minutes before serving.

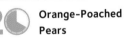

Pear, Blue Cheese and Honey Crostini

Cut a thin baguette into 8 slices and toast on one side. Cut 1 pear into thin slices and place on the untoasted side of the slices. Top with 100 g (3½ oz) crumbled dolcelatte cheese and drizzle each one with ¼ teaspoon honey. Grill for 1–2 minutes, until the cheese has melted.

Orange-Poached Pears

Combine 500 ml (17 fl oz) fresh orange juice, 75 g (3 oz) caster sugar, the grated rind of 1 orange, 3 cloves and 1 cinnamon stick in a large saucepan. Add 4 peeled, cored and quartered pears, bring to a simmer, cover and cook for about 15 minutes, until the pears are tender. Remove the pears

and boil the liquid to reduce a little. Meanwhile, whisk together 4 tablespoons mascarpone cheese, 2 tablespoons icing sugar and the grated rind of 1 orange in a bowl. Serve the pears with a dollop of the mascarpone, drizzled with a little juice and sprinkled with 2 tablespoons flaked almonds.

ITA-SWEE-GAH

Roasted Amaretti Peaches

Serves 4

4 peaches, halved and stoned
8 amaretti biscuits
1 tablespoon honey
25 g (1 oz) unsalted butter, diced

For the mascarpone cream

4 tablespoons mascarpone cheese
2 tablespoons icing sugar, sifted
2 tablespoons Amaretto liqueur
2 tablespoons toasted flaked
   almonds, to serve

- Place the peach halves, cut side up, in an ovenproof dish. Crumble the amaretti biscuits and sprinkle them into the holes in the peaches. Drizzle over the honey.

- Dot the peaches with the butter and bake in a preheated oven, 200°C (400°F), Gas Mark 6, for 15–18 minutes, until tender.

- Meanwhile, whisk together the mascarpone, icing sugar and Amaretto in a small bowl.

- Serve the peaches with a dollop of the mascarpone, sprinkled with flaked almonds.

Peachy Fruit Salad

Combine 3 stoned and chopped peaches, 325 g (11 oz) hulled and sliced strawberries, 150 g (5 oz) halved green seedless grapes and 200 g (7 oz) raspberries in a serving bowl. Whisk together the juice of 1 lime, 3 tablespoons pineapple juice, ½ teaspoon ground ginger and 2 tablespoons shredded mint leaves in a small bowl or jug. Pour over the fruit and gently toss together. Serve with a dollop of crème fraîche.

Peach and Almond Tartlets

Roll out 300 g (10 oz) shop-bought chilled puff pastry on a lightly floured work surface and cut it into four 10 x 12 cm (4 x 5 inch) rectangles. Lay them on a baking sheet. Score a border with a knife about 1 cm (½ inch) around the edge, then prick the base with a fork and brush with beaten egg. Bake in a preheated oven, 200°C (400°F), Gas Mark 6, for 10 minutes. Chop 175 g (6 oz)

marzipan and divide between the pastries. Slice 3 peaches and fan them out on top, followed by a sprinkling of 2 tablespoons flaked almonds. Return to the oven for a further 10 minutes, until golden. Meanwhile, whisk together 2 tablespoons mascarpone cheese, 2 tablespoons icing sugar and 1 tablespoon Amaretto liqueur in a bowl and serve with the tartlets.

Sweet Ricotta and Raspberries

Serves 4

450 g (14½ oz) ricotta cheese
grated rind of 2 oranges
3 tablespoons honey
350 g (11½ oz) raspberries

- Mix together the ricotta, orange rind and 2 tablespoons of the honey in a bowl.

- Gently stir in the raspberries.

- Divide the mixture between 4 glasses or small bowls.

- Drizzle with the remaining honey and serve immediately.

Sweet Ricotta Mousse

Put 360 g (11¾ oz) ricotta cheese, 180 g (6¼ oz) mascarpone cheese and 30 g (1¼ oz) caster sugar in a food processor or blender and process until well mixed. Stir in the grated rind of 2 oranges and the seeds scraped from 1 vanilla pod. Whip 450 ml (¾ pint) double cream with 2 tablespoons Amaretto liqueur, until stiff and then gently fold into the ricotta mixture. Divide between 4 glasses and chill for 10 minutes. Serve with fresh raspberries and sprigs of mint.

Baked Sweet Ricotta

Mix together 400 g (13 oz) ricotta cheese, the grated rind of 2 oranges, 75 g (3 oz) caster sugar, 125 g (4 oz) ground almonds, 125 g (4 oz) chopped peel and 4 beaten eggs in a bowl. Spoon into 4 ramekin dishes and bake in a preheated oven, 190°C (375°F), Gas Mark 5, for 20–22 minutes, until risen and golden. Meanwhile, place 350 g (11½ oz) raspberries in a saucepan with the grated rind and juice of 1 orange and 2 tablespoons caster sugar. Heat very gently for 2–3 minutes. Serve the warm berries with the baked ricotta.

Orange and Strawberry Salad

Serves 4

60 g (2¼ oz) caster sugar
100 ml (3½ fl oz) water
1 tablespoon thinly sliced
   basil leaves
150 g (5 oz) strawberries,
   hulled and halved
4 oranges

- Put the sugar and measurement water in a saucepan and bring to the boil. Simmer for 2–3 minutes and then let it cool briefly before adding the basil.

- Place the strawberries in a bowl. Peel and segment 4 oranges over the bowl to catch the juice. Add the orange segments to the strawberries.

- Pour in the syrup and serve.

2 Oranges in Marsala

Peel 4 oranges, then slice them thinly. Place them in a shallow bowl and pour over 3 tablespoons marsala (or Amaretto if preferred). Leave to marinate for 10 minutes. Place 40 g (1¾ oz) caster sugar and a small handful of chopped mint leaves in a pestle and mortar and crush them together. Sprinkle the minted sugar and 6 crushed Amaretti biscuits over the oranges and spoon into 4 serving dishes. Serve each dish with a spoonful of mascarpone cheese.

3 Caramelized Oranges

Peel 4 oranges, then slice them thinly. Place in a shallow serving dish and pour over 1 tablespoon orange liqueur. Place 115 g (3¾ oz) granulated sugar, 1 cinnamon stick and 150 ml (¼ pint) water in a saucepan. Heat, stirring, until the sugar has dissolved. Continue to simmer until the sugar starts to caramelize and turns a rich caramel colour. Pour the syrup over the oranges. Decorate with 25 g (1 oz) toasted pine nuts and 1 tablespoon chopped mint leaves.

ITA-SWEE-TAH

 # Tiramisu

Serves 4

50 g (2 oz) caster sugar
2 egg yolks
150 ml (¼ pint) strong coffee
2 tablespoons coffee liqueur
225 ml (7½ fl oz) double cream
250 g (8 oz) mascarpone cheese
225 g (7½ oz) sponge fingers
1 teaspoon cocoa powder

- Place the sugar and egg yolks in a bowl over a saucepan of simmering water and whisk for 4–5 minutes, until light and fluffy. Leave to cool slightly.

- Pour the coffee into a shallow bowl and stir in the liqueur.

- Whip the cream to soft peaks.

- Stir the mascarpone into the cooled egg yolk mixture, then gently fold in the whipped cream.

- Dip half the sponge fingers into the coffee and place them in the base of a shallow serving dish. Spread over half the cream mixture.

- Repeat with the remaining sponge fingers and cream mixture, then sift over the cocoa powder.

- Chill for 10 minutes before serving.

---

1 **Very Quick Individual Tiramisu**

Dip 12 sponge fingers into 100 ml (3½ fl oz) strong coffee and divide them between 4 glasses or small bowls. Whisk together 250 g (8 oz) mascarpone cheese with 2 tablespoons coffee liqueur and spoon over the sponge fingers. Sift over ½ teaspoon cocoa powder and serve.

2 **Tiramisu Fondue**

Put 400 g (13 oz) mascarpone cheese, 2 tablespoons strong coffee, 1 tablespoon Amaretto liqueur, 2 teaspoons cornflour and 75 g (3 oz) icing sugar in a bowl over a saucepan of simmering water. Gently stir as the mixture heats, gradually bringing it all together to form a smooth thick sauce.

When the sauce is hot, whisk 2 eggs in another bowl and pour the mascarpone mixture over, whisking constantly. Return the bowl to the heat and cook until the fondue is creamy and thick enough to dip into. Serve with chopped fruits or biscotti for dipping.

ITA-SWEE-KYE

20 Zabaglioni

Serves 4

1 vanilla pod, split lengthways
8 egg yolks
2 tablespoons caster sugar
4 tablespoons marsala
light, thin biscuits, to serve

- Scrape the seeds from the split vanilla pod and place in a bowl with the egg yolks, sugar and marsala. Whisk together with a balloon whisk.

- Place the bowl over a saucepan of simmering water, with the heat on very low, and continue to whisk for 8–10 minutes, until the mixture is very light and foamy and holds its shape.

- Spoon into 4 glasses and serve with light, thin biscuits.

---

10 Marsala Affogato Mix together 4 shots of espresso with 2 tablespoons marsala. Spoon 8 scoops of ice cream into 4 small bowls and pour over the coffee mixture while still hot. Serve sprinkled with roughly chopped dark chocolate.

30 Plums and Panettone with Zabaglioni Halve and stone 350 g (11½ oz) plums and place in a small saucepan with the juice and grated rind of 2 oranges, 65 g (2½ oz) caster sugar and 1 cinnamon stick. Simmer gently for 15 minutes, until soft.

Meanwhile, make the Zabaglioni as above. Toast 4 slices of panettone on both sides and place each one on a plate. Top with the stewed plums and finally spoon over the zabaglioni. Serve immediately.

Honeyed Figs

Serves 4

12 figs
20 g (¾ oz) unsalted butter
4 tablespoons honey
¼ teaspoon ground cinnamon

To serve (optional)

4 tablespoons mascarpone cheese
50 g (2 oz) toasted flaked
   almonds

- Cut a cross in the top of each fig, not quite cutting all the way through. Place in an ovenproof dish.

- Melt together the butter, honey and cinnamon in a saucepan and pour over the figs.

- Bake in a preheated oven, 200°C (400°F), Gas Mark 6, for 20 minutes.

- Serve the figs with a dollop of mascarpone and sprinkled with flaked almonds, if liked.

1 Figs with Honey and Cheese

Slice a ciabatta loaf into 4 by firstly cutting in half vertically and then again horizontally. Lightly toast the bread on both sides. Divide 200 g (7 oz) Gorgonzola cheese between the 4 slices. Top each one with 1 sliced fig and then drizzle over 1 tablespoon honey.

2 Fig Scones

Mix together 500 g (1 lb) plain flour, 85 g (3¼ oz) caster sugar and 30 g (1¼ oz) baking powder in a bowl. Add 85 g (3¼ oz) unsalted butter and rub in with your fingertips until the mixture ressembles breadcrumbs. Gently stir in 2 beaten eggs, 200 ml (7 fl oz) milk and 100 g (3½ oz) chopped dried figs, until you have a soft dough. Turn out on to a lightly floured work surface and roll or press out to a thickness of about 4 cm (1½ inches). Cut out 6–8 scones using a 4–5 cm (1½–2 inch) pastry cutter and place on a baking sheet. Bake in a preheated oven, 200°C (400°F), Gas Mark 6, for 15 minutes, until golden and risen. Leave to cool on a wire rack.

ITA-SWEE-GYM

30 Pear Strudel

Serves 4–6

3 pears, peeled, cored and diced
75 g (3 oz) raisins
75 g (3 oz) frozen cranberries
125 g (4 oz) caster sugar
grated rind of 1 orange
8 sheets of filo pastry
50 g (2 oz) unsalted butter,
   melted
3 tablespoons ground almonds
natural yogurt, to serve

- Place the diced pears, raisins and cranberries in a small saucepan with the sugar and orange rind and cook over a low heat for 2–3 minutes, until the pears start to soften.

- Place 1 sheet of filo on the work surface and brush with melted butter. Lay another sheet on top and brush with more butter. Repeat with the remaining sheets of filo.

- Sprinkle the buttered pastry sheets with the ground almonds.

- Spoon the pear and raisin mixture down the centre of the pastry and roll into a sausage shape, folding in the ends to enclose the fruit.

- Place on a baking sheet and brush with the remaining melted butter.

- Bake in a preheated oven, 190°C (375°F), Gas Mark 5, for 20–25 minutes, until golden.

- Cut into slices and serve with yogurt.

---

10 Poached Pears with Blackberries

Thinly slice 4 pears and poach them in 400 ml (14 fl oz) sweet red wine for 8 minutes. At the end of the cooking time, gently stir in 3 tablespoons blackberries. Serve with vanilla ice cream.

20 Ricotta-Filled Pears

Beat 125 g (4 oz) ricotta cheese with 1 tablespoon icing sugar and 1 tablespoon cocoa powder in a bowl. Stir in 50 g (2 oz) chopped dark chocolate and the grated rind of 1 orange. Peel 2 ripe pears, cut in half lengthways and remove the cores. Brush the pears with 2 tablespoons orange juice, then spoon in the ricotta filling. Serve sprinkled with mint leaves.

ITA-SWEE-BOG

Watermelon and Pineapple with Sambuca

Serves 4

½ small watermelon

1 small pineapple

4 shots of Sambuca

2 tablespoons toasted flaked almonds

4 scoops of vanilla ice cream, to serve

- Peel the watermelon and pineapple and cut into 1 cm (½ inch) thick slices.

- Stack the slices on top of each other on 4 serving plates, alternating the fruits.

- Pour 1 shot of the Sambuca over each, sprinkle with the flaked almonds and serve with a scoop of vanilla ice cream.

20 Watermelon, Pineapple and Peaches Melt 20 g (¾ oz) butter in a small frying pan and toast 2 tablespoons flaked almonds, until golden. Leave to cool. Thinly slice 4 peaches and toss together with ½ small peeled and cubed watermelon and ½ small peeled and chopped pineapple in a bowl. Mix together 2 tablespoons honey, ¼ teaspoon ground cinnamon and 5 tablespoons natural yogurt in another bowl. Divide the fruit between 4 small bowls and pour over the yogurt dressing. Sprinkle with the toasted almonds to serve.

30 Pineapple Fritters Sift 200 g (7 oz) plain flour into a bowl and then whisk in 125 ml (4 fl oz) warm water, 100 ml (3½ oz) beer, ½ tablespoon vegetable oil and ½ tablespoon marsala to make a batter. Cut 1 large cored and peeled pineapple into thick slices. Pour sunflower oil into a deep-fat fryer or large saucepan and heat to 180–190°C (350–375°F), or until a cube of bread dropped into the oil browns in 30 seconds. Whisk 2 egg whites into the batter and then dip in the pineapple slices, shaking off any excess. Working in batches if necessary, carefully drop into the hot oil. Deep-fry for 3–4 minutes, until golden all over. Remove with a slotted spoon and drain on kitchen paper. Serve scattered with torn mint leaves and dusted with caster sugar.

ITA-SWEE-SAZ

20 Amaretti Biscuits

Serves 8

2 large egg whites
175 g (6 oz) ground almonds
175 g (6 oz) caster sugar
3 teaspoons Amaretto liqueur

- Line a baking sheet with greaseproof paper. Place the egg whites in a clean, grease-free bowl and whisk with a hand-held electric whisk until soft peaks form.

- Gently fold in the ground almonds, sugar and Amaretto.

- Place teaspoons of the mixture at least 2.5 cm (1 inch) apart on the prepared baking sheet.

- Bake in a preheated oven, 160°C (325°F), Gas Mark 3, for 15 minutes, until golden.

- Leave to cool on a wire rack.

10 Raspberries with Almond Crumble

Place 400 g (13 oz) raspberries in a gratin dish. Mix together 40 g (1¾ oz) melted butter, 20 g (¾ oz) caster sugar and 125 g (4 oz) ground almonds in a bowl. Roughly spread the almond mixture over the fruit and cook under a preheated medium-hot grill for 5–6 minutes, until golden. Serve with single cream.

30 Almond Shortbread

Cream together 100 g (3½ oz) softened unsalted butter and 50 g (2 oz) caster sugar, until light and fluffy. Stir in 100 g (3½ oz) self-raising flour, 25 g (1 oz) ground almonds and a few drops of Amaretto liqueur. Place 8–10 walnut-sized balls of the mixture at least 2.5 cm (1 inch) apart on a greased baking sheet. Press each one down lightly with a fork and then bake in a preheated oven, 180°C (350°F), Gas Mark 4, for 15 minutes, until golden. Leave to cool on a wire rack.

Sweet Berry Pizzas

Serves 4

500 g (1 lb) strong bread flour, plus extra for dusting

4 tablespoons caster sugar

7 g (¼ oz) sachet dried yeast

a pinch of salt

1 tablespoon olive oil

300 ml (½ pint) warm water

300 g (10 oz) full-fat cream cheese

3 large egg yolks

2–3 drops of vanilla extract

400 g (13 oz) fresh berries

175 g (6 oz) soft light brown sugar

25 g (1 oz) plain flour

50 g (2 oz) unsalted butter, melted

- To make the dough, place the flour, 2 tablespoons of the sugar, the yeast and salt in a large bowl and mix together. Make a well in the centre. Stir in the olive oil and most of the measurement water. Mix together with your hand, gradually adding more water, if necessary, until you have a soft, but not sticky dough.

- Turn the dough out on to a floured work surface and knead for 5–10 minutes, until the dough is smooth and elastic.

- Divide the dough into 4 pieces and roll out to 15 cm (6 inch) circles, then place on 2 large baking sheets.

- Mix together the cream cheese, egg yolks, vanilla extract and remaining caster sugar and spread over the pizza bases. Top with the berries.

- Mix together the brown sugar, plain flour and melted butter in a bowl and sprinkle over the berries.

- Bake in a preheated oven, 220°C (425°F), Gas Mark 7, for 12–15 minutes, until golden.

---

1 **Sweet Pitta Breads**
Toast 4 pitta breads on both sides. Mix together 200 g (7 oz) cream cheese with 2 tablespoons light brown sugar in a bowl and spread over the pitta breads. Sprinkle each one with 50 g (2 oz) raspberries and drizzle with 2 teaspoons honey. Cook under a preheated hot grill for 2–3 minutes and serve sprinkled with 1 teaspoon toasted sesame seeds.

2 **Cheat's Sweet Calzones**
Mix together 200 g (7 oz) cream cheese, 1 egg yolk and 2 tablespoons caster sugar in a bowl. Lay 4 flour tortillas on the work surface and spread half of each one with the cream cheese mixture, leaving a 2.5 cm (1 inch) clean edge. Add 200 g (7 oz) hulled and sliced strawberries and a small handful of blueberries. Brush beaten egg around the clean edges of each tortilla and then fold over the other halves to make semicircles. Press down the edges to seal. Heat 25 g (1 oz) butter and 1 tablespoon olive oil in a frying pan and fry the tortillas for 3–4 minutes on each side, until golden.

ITA-SWEE-PAO

Apple and Parmesan Tartlets

Serves 4

flour, for dusting

175 g (6 oz) shop-bought chilled puff pastry

2 teaspoons soft light brown sugar

2 tart dessert apples, peeled, cored and sliced

2 teaspoons honey

40 g (1¾ oz) Parmesan cheese, grated

For the mascarpone cream (optional)

4 tablespoons mascarpone cheese

grated rind and juice of ½ lemon

1 teaspoon dark muscovado sugar

- Line a baking sheet with greaseproof paper. Roll the pastry out on a lightly floured work surface and cut out four 10 x 12 cm (4 x 5 inch) rectangles. Place them on the baking sheet and sprinkle with the light brown sugar.

- Arrange the apple slices in a line on each rectangle of pastry. Drizzle each one with the honey and then sprinkle over the grated Parmesan.

- Bake in a preheated oven, 200°C (400°F), Gas Mark 6, for 12–14 minutes, until golden.

- Meanwhile, to make the mascarpone cream, if using, whisk together the mascarpone, lemon rind and juice and muscovado sugar in a bowl.

- Serve each tartlet with a dollop of mascarpone cream, if liked.

Toffee Apples with Rice Pudding

Melt 100 g (3½ oz) butter and 3 tablespoons honey in a saucepan. Add 4 peeled, cored and sliced apples and warm for 3–4 minutes in the syrup. Serve the toffee apples spooned over a 425 g (15 oz) can rice pudding, warmed through according to the instructions on the can.

Apple Fritters

Sift together 150 g (5 oz) self-raising flour and 1 teaspoon ground cinnamon in a bowl. Stir in 60 g (2¼ oz) caster sugar. Whisk in 190 ml (7 fl oz) apple juice to make a thick coating batter, slightly thicker than the consistency of double cream. Pour sunflower oil into a deep-fat fryer or large saucepan and heat to 180–190°C (350–375°F), or until a cube of bread dropped into the oil browns in 30 seconds. Peel and core 4 apples, remove the tops and bottoms and then slice into 1 cm (½ inch) thick rings. Dip the apple slices into the batter and then, working in batches, carefully drop into the hot oil. Deep-fry for 1–2 minutes, until golden. Remove with a slotted spoon and drain on kitchen paper. Dust with icing sugar and serve with mascarpone.

Creamy Peach and Banana Smoothies

Serves 4

1 large banana

3 peaches, peeled, halved
  and stoned

2 pieces of stem ginger

200 g (7 oz) natural yogurt

150 ml (¼ pint) milk, plus extra
  if needed

- Place the banana, peaches, stem ginger, yogurt and milk in a food processor or blender and blend until smooth, adding more milk if necessary.

- Pour into 4 glasses and serve immediately.

---

2 Peaches with Spiced Ricotta

Toast 2 tablespoons ground almonds in a dry-frying pan for 2–3 minutes and then stir them into 200 g (7 oz) ricotta cheese with ¼ teaspoon ground cinnamon, the grated rind of ½ orange and 2 diced pieces of stem ginger. Halve and stone 4 peaches, then place in an ovenproof dish. Spoon the filling into each one and cook under a preheated hot grill for 4–5 minutes.

3 Raisin-Stuffed Peaches

Place 100 g (3½ oz) raisins in a bowl and pour over 125 ml (4 fl oz) rum. Leave to stand for 10 minutes. Place 1 halved and stoned peach in a food processor or blender and process to a pulp. Stir in 1 tablespoon caster sugar and the marinated raisins. Place another 4 halved and stoned peaches in an ovenproof dish and spoon the peach pulp and raisins into the centre of each one. Pour 125 ml (4 fl oz) white wine around the peaches. Bake in a preheated oven, 200°C (400°F), Gas Mark 6, for 15 minutes, sprinkling over 2 tablespoons flaked almonds for the last minute of cooking. Serve with vanilla ice cream or crème fraîche.

Biscotti

Serves 4

110 g (3¾ oz) caster sugar

110 g (3¾ oz) plain flour, plus extra for dusting

1 teaspoon baking powder

grated rind of 1 lemon

50 g (2 oz) blanched almonds

15 g (½ oz) dried cranberries

1 egg, beaten

- Place all of the ingredients in a bowl and, using your hands, bring them together to make a stiff dough.

- Turn out on to a floured work surface and roll into a sausage shape about 28 cm (11 inches) long. Place on a baking sheet and bake in a preheated oven, 220°C (425°F), Gas Mark 7, for 15 minutes.

- Remove from the oven, leave to cool for 2–3 minutes and then gently slice into biscotti.

- Lay the biscotti flat on the baking sheet, return to the oven and cook for a further 2–3 minutes to crisp.

- Leave to cool on a wire rack.

---

1 Creamy Peach, Cranberry and Raspberry Biscotti Puddings

Whizz 10 ready-made biscotti in a food processor or a blender and then mix with 40 g (1¾ oz) melted butter. Press this into the bottom of 4 ramekin dishes. Divide 2 halved, stoned and chopped peaches, 50 g (2 oz) dried cranberries and 100 g (3½ oz) raspberries between the dishes. Spoon 2 tablespoons natural yogurt into each ramekin and sprinkle with 2 teaspoons dark muscovado sugar. Chill for 2 minutes before serving.

2 Cranberry and Almond Scones

Sift together 225 g (7½ oz) self-raising flour and a pinch of salt in a large bowl. Add 75 g (3 oz) unsalted butter and rub in with your fingertips until the mixture resembles breadcrumbs. Stir in 40 g (1¾ oz) caster sugar, 25 g (1 oz) dried cranberries and 25 g (1 oz) flaked almonds. Beat together 1 egg and 2 tablespoons buttermilk and mix into the flour mixture, until you have a soft dough. Turn out on to a lightly floured work surface and roll or press out to a thickness of 2.5 cm (1 inch). Cut out 10 scones using a 5 cm (2 inch) pastry cutter and place on a baking sheet. Bake in a preheated oven, 220°C (425°F), Gas Mark 7, for 10–12 minutes, until golden and risen. Leave to cool on a wire rack.

30 Honeyed Fig Fool

Serves 4

250 g (8 oz) figs
grated rind of 1 orange
3 tablespoons fresh orange juice
2 tablespoons honey
250 g (8 oz) thick natural yogurt

To serve

1 tablespoon toasted flaked
  almonds
amaretti biscuits

- Place the figs, orange rind and juice and honey in a small saucepan and simmer for 12–15 minutes, until soft and creamy. Leave to cool slightly.

- Place the figs in a food processor or blender and blend until smooth. Stir in the yogurt, not mixing too thoroughly, to give a marbled effect.

- Spoon into 4 small bowls or glasses and serve sprinkled with flaked almonds, and with amaretti biscuits for dipping.

---

1 **Fruit Kebabs**
Thread 200 g (7 oz) hulled and halved strawberries, 3 stoned peaches, cut into wedges, and 4 quartered figs on to wooden kebab skewers. Melt 50 g (2 oz) dark chocolate with 2 tablespoons double cream and 1 teaspoon honey in a saucepan, then drizzle over the kebabs. Serve sprinkled with 2 tablespoons toasted flaked almonds.

---

2 **Strawberry and Fig Bruschetta**
Toast 8 slices of ciabatta on both sides. Stir 4 tablespoons honey, 2 teaspoons grated lemon rind and 2 teaspoons lemon juice in a small saucepan and cook until the honey has melted a little. Stir in 125 g (4 oz) hulled and halved strawberries and 3 quartered figs, cook for 1 minute and then remove from the heat. Spoon ½ tablespoon mascarpone cheese on to each piece of toast and spoon over the strawberries and figs. Serve immediately.

ITA-SWEE-QYK

30 Ricotta Pancakes with Oranges and Figs

Serves 4

100 ml (3½ fl oz) milk
250 g (8 oz) ricotta cheese
75 g (3 oz) plain flour
½ teaspoon baking powder
2 eggs, separated
1 tablespoon caster sugar
25 g (1 oz) butter
2 oranges
2 teaspoons honey
3 figs, quartered

- Place the milk, ricotta, flour, baking powder, egg yolks and sugar in a food processor or blender and process until smooth.

- Whisk the egg whites in a bowl with a hand-held electric whisk, until soft peaks form, then fold this into the processed batter.

- Melt the butter in a nonstick frying pan, drop spoonfuls of the batter into the pan and cook for 2–3 minutes on each side, until golden. Cook in batches, keeping the pancakes warm until all the batter is used.

- Peel and segment the oranges over a bowl to catch the juice. Place the juice and honey in a saucepan and warm through.

- Serve 3 pancakes per person on a plate with orange segments, pieces of fig and the juice and honey poured over the top.

---

10 Souffléd Orange Omelette

Whisk 2 egg whites in a bowl with a hand-held electric whisk, until soft peaks form. In a separate bowl, whisk 2 egg yolks with 1½ tablespoons caster sugar. Fold the egg whites into the egg yolks. Melt 5 g (¼ oz) butter in a flameproof omelette pan and pour in the eggs. Leave to cook over a low heat for 2–3 minutes, then drop in the segments of 1 orange. Sift over 1 teaspoon icing sugar and cook under a preheated hot grill for 1–2 minutes, until slightly golden.

20 Caramelized Oranges with Sweet Ricotta

Pare the rind from 2 oranges and cut into fine threads. Peel and segment 6 large oranges, reserving the juice, placing them both on a heatproof serving platter. Slowly cook 250 g (8 oz) caster sugar in a saucepan over a medium heat, until it starts to melt. When the sugar starts to caramelize pour in 200 ml (7 fl oz) hot water and reduce the heat to low. Add the orange rind and simmer for 5 minutes. Pour the hot syrup over the orange segments. Mix together 350 g (11½ oz) ricotta with 1 tablespoon honey in a bowl. Serve the oranges with a dollop of the ricotta cheese and sprinkled with 2 tablespoons toasted pine nuts.

ITA-SWEE-JOY

Amaretto Apricot Dessert

Serves 4

400 g (13 oz) can apricots
in syrup
2 tablespoons Amaretto liqueur
4 scoops of vanilla ice cream
8 Amaretti biscuits, crushed

- Drain the syrup from the apricots into a saucepan and simmer to reduce a little, then stir in the Amaretto.

- Divide the apricots between 4 bowls and pour over the warm syrup.

- Add a scoop of vanilla ice cream to each dish and serve sprinkled with the crushed amaretti biscuits.

Vanilla-Roasted Apricots and Figs with Spiced Mascarpone

Cut a cross in the top of 8 figs, making sure not to cut all the way through. Place them in a roasting tin with 300 g (10 oz) halved and stoned apricots. Scrape the seeds from 1 split vanilla pod, then cut the pod into 3 pieces. Put both in a pestle and mortar with 50 g (2 oz) golden caster sugar and grind together until well mixed. Sprinkle the sugar over the fruit and roast in a preheated oven, 200°C (400°F), Gas Mark 6, for 12–15 minutes, until starting to caramelize. Meanwhile, blend 3 pieces of stem ginger and 4 teaspoons ginger syrup in a small blender, then whisk into 200 g (7 oz) mascarpone cheese. Serve the fruits topped with a dollop of the mascarpone and a sprinkling of ground nutmeg.

Apricot Pancakes with Orange Mascarpone

Sift 140 g (5 oz) self-raising flour and a pinch of bicarbonate of soda into a bowl. Stir in 25 g (1 oz) caster sugar. Beat together 1 egg and 150 ml (¼ pint) milk in a separate bowl and then whisk it into the flour until smooth. Stir in 40 g (1¾ oz) chopped dried apricots. Grate the rind of 1 orange, then segment over a bowl to catch the juice. Stir the rind, juice and segments into 250 g (8 oz) mascarpone cheese with 1 tablespoon orange liqueur. Heat 1 teaspoon olive oil in a frying pan and drop in 4 tablespoons of batter. Cook for 1 minute and then flip over and cook for another minute. Repeat with the remaining batter. Serve 3–4 warm pancakes per person with a large dollop of the mascarpone.

ITA-SWEE-PIJ

Mixed Peel Cassata

Serves 4

285 g (9½ oz) ready-made Madeira cake
300 g (10 oz) ricotta cheese
60 g (2¼ oz) chopped mixed peel
25 g (1 oz) dark chocolate, chopped
25 g (1 oz) caster sugar
2 tablespoons Amaretto liqueur

- Line a 500 g (1 lb) loaf tin with clingfilm, leaving enough hanging over the sides to be able to fold across the top.

- Slice the Madeira cake into 3 slices horizontally.

- Mix together the ricotta, mixed peel, chocolate and sugar in a bowl.

- Place 1 slice of cake in the base of the loaf tin. Spoon half the ricotta mixture on top and spread to cover the cake.

- Repeat with a second slice of cake and the remaining ricotta.

- Cover with the remaining slice of cake and sprinkle over the Amaretto.

- Pull the clingfilm over the top to seal, press down gently and then place in the freezer for 20 minutes to set.

1. Pears with Mixed Peel Ricotta

Peel, core and slice 4 pears and place in 4 small bowls. Stir 1 tablespoon Amaretto liqueur and 2 tablespoons chopped mixed peel into 150 g (5 oz) ricotta cheese. Divide between the 4 bowls and drizzle 1 teaspoon honey over each one. Serve immediately.

2. Mixed Peel and Chocolate Scones

Sift 225 g (7½ oz) self-raising flour into a bowl. Add 75 g (3 oz) butter and rub in with your fingertips until the mixture resembles breadcrumbs. Stir in 40 g (1¾ oz) sugar, 1 tablespoon chopped dark chocolate and ½ tablespoon chopped mixed peel. Beat together 1 egg and 2 tablespoons buttermilk and mix into the flour mixture, until you have a soft dough. Turn out on to a floured work surface and press or roll out to a thickness of 2.5 cm (1 inch). Cut out 10 scones using a 5 cm (2 inch) pastry cutter and place on a baking sheet. Bake in a preheated oven, 220°C (425°F), Gas Mark 7, for 10–12 minutes, until risen.

ITA-SWEE-GOL

Chocolate Amaretti Puddings

Serves 4

125 g (4 oz) unsalted butter, plus extra, melted, for greasing

1 teaspoon cocoa powder, sifted

125 g (4 oz) dark chocolate, chopped

3 large eggs

125 g (4 oz) caster sugar

35 g (1¼ oz) plain flour

50 g (2 oz) amaretti biscuits, crumbled

- Brush 4 large ramekin dishes with the melted butter and shake in the cocoa powder to coat.

- Melt the chocolate and butter in a bowl over a saucepan of simmering water.

- Meanwhile, whisk together the eggs and sugar until light and fluffy.

- Stir the chocolate, flour and crumbled amaretti biscuits into the egg mixture.

- Divide between the prepared ramekin dishes and bake in the preheated oven, 190 °C (375 °F), Gas Mark 5, for 12–15 minutes, until they have risen.

1 Chocolate and Amaretto Dessert

Melt together 60 g (2¼ oz) dark chocolate, 30 g (1¼ oz) unsalted butter and 30 g (1¼ oz) golden syrup in a small saucepan, stirring occasionally, until you have a smooth chocolate sauce. Place a few amaretti biscuits into 4 ramekin dishes, sprinkle ½ teaspoon Amaretto liqueur over each and then pour the chocolate sauce over the top. Serve with a dollop of crème fraîche and a sprinkling of cocoa powder.

2 Quick Chocolate Mousse

Heat 300 ml (½ pint) double cream in a small saucepan until boiling. Stir in 200 g (7 oz) chopped dark chocolate and stir until melted. Pour into a bowl and place this bowl in another bowl of ice to rapidly cool. Pour in 300 ml (½ pint) double cream, 1–2 tablespoons Amaretto liqueur and 10–12 crumbled amaretti biscuits. Whisk until soft peaks form. Spoon into glasses or small bowls and serve.

Index

Page references in *italics* indicate photographs

Acknowledgements

Recipes by: **Joy Skipper**
Executive Editor: **Eleanor Maxfield**
Senior Editor: **Leanne Bryan**
Copy Editor: **Abi Waters**
Art Direction: **Tracy Killick Art Direction and Design**
Original Design Concept: **www.gradedesign.com**
Designer: **Sally Bond for Tracy Killick Art Direction and Design**
Photographer: **Lis Parsons**
Home Economist: **Joy Skipper**
Prop Stylist: **Liz Hippisley**
Production Controller: **Davide Pontiroli**